PROVENCE
& THE CÔTE D'AZUR

THE HELM FRENCH REGIONAL GUIDES

Series Editor: **Arthur Eperon**

Auvergne and the Massif Central
Rex Grizell

The Dordogne and Lot
Arthur and Barbara Eperon

Languedoc and Roussillon
Andrew Sanger

The Loire Valley
Arthur and Barbara Eperon

PROVENCE
& THE CÔTE D'AZUR
Roger Macdonald

Photographs by Joe Cornish

CHRISTOPHER HELM
London

© 1989 Roger Macdonald

Photographs by Joe Cornish
Line illustrations by David Saunders
Maps by Oxford Cartographers

Christopher Helm (Publishers) Ltd,
Imperial House, 21-25 North Street,
Bromley, Kent BR1 1SD

ISBN 0-7470-2207-0

Title illustration: St. André's Fort, once the
gateway to Avignon.

Typeset by Leaper and Gard, Bristol
Printed and bound in Italy

Contents

1
Introduction

If J.R. Tolkien had come to Provence, he might never have invented Middle Earth. For all the ingredients of a magic land are here in abundance: legends, monsters, wicked Lords of the Ruins if not of the Rings, sorcerers and saints, chasms and cascades, and beyond the dark valleys the shimmering sea.

After the Romans abandoned their favourite *Provincia*, leaving behind great monuments to their power and presence, Provence, if not quite Middle Earth, became a series of middle kingdoms, buffer states

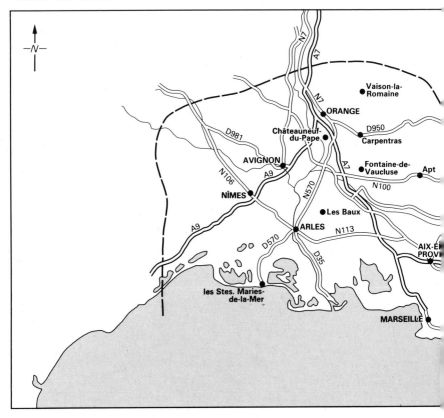

coveted by Italian princes, the King of France and the Holy Roman Emperor. For a while it displaced Rome as the residence of the Pope, and remained proudly independent until the 15th century. Even then it took France a further 370 years to acquire all its southern borders, apart from the pocket Principality of Monaco.

Provence, then, has a unique place in European history and culture. Augustus, Mary Magdalene, Charlemagne, Nostradamus, Petrarch, Mirabeau, Napoléon, the Marquis de Sade, the Count of Monte Cristo, the Man in the Iron Mask and the Man Who Broke the Bank at Monte Carlo each contributed to its identity.

The improbability of its distant past is matched only by the development of Provence as the playground of Europe, first as a precarious winter refuge for British invalids, then of British and European society. It took the innovative drive of the Americans to make the Riviera a summer paradise, where holidays in the grand manner have survived all the distortions of mass tourism.

Only in Provence can visitors gaze in awe at Roman ruins, be swallowed up by the time warp of the Provençal countryside, and engage in the vibrant pleasures of the Riviera, all in a single visit. Such contrasts are its ceaseless and captivating charm.

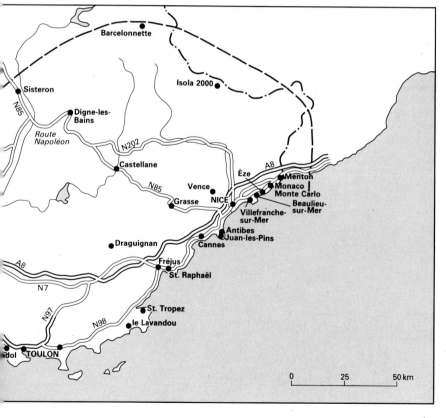

2
History

The earthly paradise that became Provence and the Côte d'Azur began with a piece of Biblical larceny. For according to legend, when Adam and Eve were expelled from the Garden of Eden, risking the wrath of their escort out of Heaven, the Angel of the Flaming Sword, she plucked and hid a lemon from a tree. The fallen pair found Earth a bleak and desolate contrast but at last happened upon a fertile spot sheltered by tall mountains and lapped by a clear azure sea. Here, at what became Menton, Eve took out the lemon which, unlike the ancestors of man, retained its immortality, and planted it in the ground. Soon the valleys and the slopes of the hills were covered with lemon trees that bloomed and bore fruit all the year round, a little corner of Eden.

In reality much of pre-historic Provence could not sustain life: the ground was simply too rough and too barren to support the great mammals such as the bison and the mammoth. The summer heat would have killed off the woolly elephant long before the hunters. The best that they could have hoped to find would have been red deer or rabbit. Through sheer force of circumstances, therefore, the huntsman ceased to be a mere collector of food and became a food producer, by engaging in agriculture and animal husbandry. He moved from pasture to pasture between the rich coastal strip and the lower Alps, keeping out the winter chill by building *bories* on the plateaux, the first roofed, free-standing stone dwellings.

However the transformation of Provence into a sophisticated trading centre rests with the Greeks from Asia Minor, the Phocaeans, who arrived about 600BC and founded Massalia, on the site of present day Marseille. It was probably called Massalia after two Ligurian words — *mas* or 'house' and *salia* after the Salians, who lived there. *Mas*, of course, has found its way into common Provençal usage as a unique style of stone dwelling, constructed with a minimum of mortar. The Phocaeans introduced cultivation of the vine and the olive, and persuaded some of the local tribes, the Ligurians, to use money instead of barter and even to worship Greek gods. But these were not echoes of the epic adventures of Jason and the Argonauts; rather, as Plato disparagingly put it, 'like frogs and ants around a pool'.

As Massalia's influence increased, it forged an alliance with the rising power of the Romans. In 218BC the Massalian fleet prevented Hannibal from landing at the eastern end of the Riviera and he

A Provençal borie adapted as a garden wall

by endless supplies of slave labour, to move its legions from one end of the Empire to the other. Provence was a natural crossroads. The *Via Aurelia* linked Italy to Spain, by way of Nice, Fréjus, Aix and Nîmes, following the line of the present-day Route Nationale 7. It was joined by the Alpine *Via Domitia*, by way of Sisteron, Apt and Pont Julien; and by the *Via Agrippa*, linking Orange, Avignon and Arles.

As much of inland Provence was short of water, the Romans devised great aqueducts such as the Pont du Gard to carry supplies over prodigious distances. They gave Roman towns the benefit of public baths, fountains and sometimes even sewage disposal on a scale otherwise quite impossible.

Rome built at a remarkable pace, less by sheer weight of numbers than by planning and innovation, such as

A Provençal "mas": minimum mortar, maximum strength

was compelled instead to enter Italy by way of the Rhône and the Alps.

The Romans later returned the favour, sending an army to repel the Celtic Salians when they threatened Massalia. The Romans, however, were not content to destroy Entremont, the Salian capital: they turned it into a fortified settlement, *Aquae Sextiae*, which became Aix-en-Provence. Twenty years later, in 102BC, the savage Teutons brought their women and children in a huge train of leather-curtained wagons, all the way from the Baltic. The Roman general Marius fell on them unexpectedly at the foot of what afterwards became known as Montagne St Victoire. In all 100,000 Germans are said to have been slain.

Rome rarely kept huge armies in the field because of the expense, but relied on superb communications, roads built

3

mortar, cement and lead piping. They borrowed the best of Greek architecture, brought in Greek freedmen, and constructed amphitheatres, theatres and temples. Provence became the most Romanised part of Gaul, the favoured choice of exiles: Provincia Romana, *the* Province.

For a time Massalia, renamed Massilia, was allowed to keep her fleet and her influence over the coast from Monaco to the Rhône. But when in 49BC the city backed Pompei, during the Roman Civil War, the victorious Caesar took away its walls, its weapons, and most of its ships and possessions. Thereafter Arles, the granary of Rome, was the pre-eminent city in Provence, and in the 4th century AD became, under Constantine, capital of the whole of Gaul.

Caesar governed the region for seven years, pushing out the frontiers of the Empire. The Roman language gradually displaced all native tongues apart from Basque and Breton, and in Provence, provided the basis of its unique dialect. Provençal derives directly from vulgar Latin, and is known as 'la langue d'oc', giving its name to the departement of Languedoc. 'Oc' was the word originally used for 'yes' in southern France, whereas elsewhere 'yes' was 'oil' and the French spoken in the remainder of the territory accordingly was known as 'la langue d'oil'.

In the end Rome's territorial ambitions proved her undoing. Under pressure from the Barbarians, Roman rule in Provence collapsed. After centuries of fighting, the region eventually fell to the Franks, who rebuffed first

Cannes: Lord Brougham's little fishing village

Attila the Hun and later the Saracens, but only at the cost of reducing Provence to total devastation.

The great Frankish king, Charlemagne, visited Provence in 776. Six feet tall, he was an imposing figure, with large, piercing eyes and a huge sense of humour. Such was his sway over his followers, that at his death they interred him in Aachen Cathedral in a quite macabre fashion: sitting on a marble throne, a crown on his head, a globe in one hand, a sceptre in the other, the imperial mantle draped over his shoulders.

Charlemagne revived the Holy Roman Empire and in 800 was crowned by the Pope at St Peter's in Rome. Soon bishops and counts ruled in Charlemagne's name over most of his territories, establishing the social and economic institutions of great domains, vassalage and serfdom, which endured until the French Revolution.

It was, however, a precarious peace. The Saracens continued to plunder Provence from the sea, forcing the inhabitants to shut themselves up at night in fortified hill settlements, the so-called 'perched' villages. The Moors were the undisputed masters of the Massif des Maures north of Hyères, a mountain range full of deep ravines and impenetrable forests, until the capture in 973 of their principal stronghold, Le Frassinet, the La Garde-Freinet of today. Their defeat however left a vacuum that was filled by the warrior Lords of Les Baux, a natural fortress north-east of Arles. In the course of the next century, they extended their rule as far as Orange in the north and the Camargue in the south.

In the 11th and 12th centuries Provence rose above its troubles. Huge forests were reduced and land planted, the population increased, trade and travel were restored with the revival of fairs and pilgrimages. The Cistercian order built superb monasteries, such as Sénanque, using the great innovation of stone vaulting.

Provence continued as an independent fief of the Empire, more often than not part of Burgundy, a ramshackle kingdom that changed shape and size so frequently that it was a ready-made fictional location for future comic opera. In the same way Provence was the prize in a medieval tug-of-war between some larger-than-life barons: the Counts of Toulouse, the Counts of Barcelona, and Charles I of Anjou. But whoever happened to be their liege-lord, the peasants lived in abject poverty, in sharp contrast to the flowering of chivalry and extravagant, formalised society, taken to extremes in the Court of Love at Les Baux.

The Albigensian Crusade, launched to eradicate heresy in south-west France, also destroyed the power of the Duchy of Toulouse. Among the territory ceded by the Duchy, given as a reward to the Papacy for its support, was the obscure Comtat Venaissin, near Avignon, on the banks of the Rhône. In 1305 Pope Clement V, a Frenchman by birth, determined to distance himself from the anarchy of Italy by moving the Papal Court to Avignon. For almost 70 years Provence, a political backwater, became a centre of European diplomacy.

The presence of the Popes in Avignon for much of the 14th century saved their territories from ruin during the One Hundred Years' War. But when the War spilled over into Provence, the obscure Italian Republic of Savoy, a hitherto landlocked state, seized the opportunity in 1388 to annex Nice and its surrounding coastline.

In the 15th century Provence acquired a monarch, Good King René, who kept his title as the exiled King of Naples. For almost 40 years he presided over the golden age of Provence. In many ways René was ahead of his time, the arch-typical Renaissance man: lawyer, linguist, musician and mathematician. Ironically for someone constantly close to bankruptcy, he introduced the key to future Provençal prosperity, the silkworm and the Muscat grape. René was succeeded in 1480 by the weak and sickly Charles of Maine, who survived only long enough to put his signature to a will that René, the great romantic, had drawn up for him: leaving Provence to the royal house of France.

In the mid-16th century the Religious Wars set Catholic against Protestant in a series of atrocities. Some of the worst occurred in the Lubéron hills of Provence, where the Vaudois, a fundamentalist sect, were rooted out mercilessly by the Catholic barons who burned villages and their inhabitants with equal zeal. A century later, absentee landlords were a recipe for rural stagnation and social discontent. But the seeds of Revolution, once sown, bore fruit slowly, and were nurtured by accidents of history. In 1720 a ship from the Levant brought the plague first to Marseille and quickly to the rest of Provence, where more than 90,000 died. The papal enclave of Venaissin tried in vain to keep out the pestilence by constructing a wall 60 miles long, manned by sentry posts. It was followed by a succession of severe winters that ruined the harvest and resulted in inflated grain prices in Marseille and Toulon. Poverty gave way to starvation, and a growing realisation of the flagrant inequalities between rich and poor.

As the Revolution gathered momentum, in 1792 Marseille sent 500 volunteers to Paris. Tired and footsore, they raised their spirits in the Parisian streets by singing a battle song written by a young Alsatian staff officer for troops on the Rhine:

Allons, enfants de la patrie
Le jour de gloire est arrivé

which was taken up by cheering spectators and spread like wildfire. Before long, it was the battle hymn of the Revolution, known, because of how it had come to Paris, as La Marseillaise.

The execution of Louis XVI in January 1793 caused a feeling of widespread revulsion in Provence, where Toulon opened its harbour to the enemies of the Revolution, the Anglo-Spanish fleet. However, a 24-year-old artillery lieutenant from Corsica, one Napoléon Bonaparte, realised that a single fort on a peninsula controlled access to the harbour. He was allowed to lead the attack, which was entirely successful, giving the British and Spanish little option but to withdraw. A sharp contrast to Napoleon's landing at Golfe-Juan in 1815, ending his exile in Elba, when he received a hostile almost contemptuous reception. It was only when he took the road to Grenoble that his old troops rallied to his standard.

Napoléon's final eclipse proved the signal for old scores to be settled, and Bonapartists were murdered in Avignon and Marseille. The so-called 'White Terror' proved extremely damaging for Provence, setting the region apart from the rest of France. The wine and silkworm industries so imaginatively created by Good King

St. Tropez

René were destroyed by disease. Only Marseille flourished because of the improvement in steam navigation and the opening, in 1869, of the Suez Canal, a shorter route to the East.

Sea travel may have become faster, but travel by land to Nice remained slow, uncomfortable and precarious for much of the 19th century. Relations between France and Savoy were so bad that at least three separate bridges across the River Var, which marked the border, had been deliberately destroyed by one side or the other. In the absence of a bridge, *gaieurs* carried passengers across on their shoulders for a fee, and guided the empty coach to safety with their poles.

The Var was not the only hazard faced by early travellers. What roads did exist, were described by an Italian diplomat as 'quite as bumpy as a marriage bed'. Most of the early visitors put up with these formidable obstacles because of their chronic state of health: many were sufferers from advanced tuberculosis, desperate for a cure. In December 1834, the Lord Chancellor of England, Lord Brougham, taking his daughter to the Mediterranean on account of her poor health, was prevented from crossing the frontier because of cholera in Provence. Instead he became captivated by Cannes, still a tiny fishing village. Within a fortnight of his arrival he had negotiated some land and began building a villa, regularly spending his winters there for the next 30 years.

The frontier disappeared in 1860 when Nice and Roquebrune voted to become part of France, and Menton was purchased from the Prince of Monaco, who as usual had pressing creditors. He received four million francs from the French government, which as the British consul in Nice observed, seemed 'a large sum to pay for a lot of lemons'.

A condition of the sale of Menton was an agreement by the Prince of Monaco to allow the railway route from Cannes to Genoa to pass across his territory, which, although he did not appreciate it at the time, was to prove the salvation of his ailing casino and impecunious Principality. The line reached Cannes in 1863, Nice a year later, Monaco and Menton in 1868. The transformation was spectacular. The journey from London could now be accomplished between breakfast on the first day and supper on the second, previously unthinkable. From Nice to Monaco by rail took a mere 20 minutes, compared to a four-hour bumpy coach journey or up to five hours by boat. When the first trains arrived in Monaco, there were only two hotels in the Principality; by the turn of the century, there were fifty.

The train was fast, but not yet comfortable, except, that is, for the likes of princes. The crowned heads of Europe vied with one another to create personalised rolling stock of elegance and grandeur. It all put the Mediterranean within reach, even for the Russians, in many ways the pioneers of international train travel. Czar Alexander II arrived at Nice with his Czarina by rail in 1864, barely a week after the line had been opened.

The visits of the Czar were soon eclipsed by the royal patronage of the Queen of England. If Queen Victoria did not exactly put the South of France on the map, her presence made it the mecca of high society. From 1882 the Queen made nine pilgrimages to the South, invariably travelling down during the second week of March, and returning during the last week of April. She held audiences for other European monarchs and greeted the citizens of France as though they were her own subjects. To a country that had disposed of two kings and two emperors, it must have seemed a little bizarre.

The Prince of Wales, too, was a frequent visitor to the Riviera, living on his yacht, an earlier *Britannia,* in order to distance himself from his mother as far as was decently possible.

The deep blue Mediterranean sea also provided the title of a book on the South of France published in 1887 by Stephen Liégeard, lawyer, politician, writer and poet. The book received a prize from the Academie Française, a glowing review in *Le Figaro,* and soon the ultimate accolade: a permanent place in the French language. It was called *La Côte d'Azur.*

The wonderful colours of the coastline, and its brilliant light, also attracted the greatest French artists. It was perhaps not surprising that Paul Cézanne, the leading Post-Impressionist, should spend most of his life in Provence, as he was born at Aix; but Van Gogh, Renoir and Picasso also all moved to the South.

The Côte d'Azur was now the very height of fashion. Luxury rail travel no longer remained exclusive to princes. In 1897, to complement their sleeping car service, Wagon Lit opened the Riviera Palace in Monte Carlo, described with almost justifiable hyperbole as 'the most luxurious hotel in the world'. Soon there were Pullman coaches to the South of France direct from St. Petersburg, Berlin, Vienna, Amsterdam, Hamburg and Rome. But in 1914 it all ended with the guns of

August. The Russians and the Germans left the Riviera, most never to return.

When the lights went back on in Europe, it almost seemed as if nothing had changed. The Riviera was still a winter playground, though now patronised more by the rich and the powerful than by an elite royal circle. From December, 1922 they were able to travel from Calais in new blue and gold sumptuous sleeping cars which gave rise to the famous name, *Le Train Bleu*. Many of the passengers were Americans, who wittingly or unwittingly, extended the Riviera's season, if for no other reason than that crossing the Atlantic was much more agreeable in summer than in winter.

Hitherto, in the early 1920s, hotel grounds were often littered in summer with mattresses out for an airing, and the hotels themselves were full of workmen and decorators. Only one remained open in Menton, while in Antibes in August the town telephone exchange closed for two hours at lunchtime and altogether after 7pm.

If one person could be said to have set in motion a course of events that switched the seasons in the South of France, then it was the American Broadway composer, Cole Porter. He discovered Antibes when it was still largely unknown, and introduced it to a couple who were to transform Antibes from a winter to a summer resort: Gerald and Sara Murphy, cultural socialites from Boston. In 1923 they purchased a house just below the Antibes lighthouse, renaming it Villa America. Their guest list read like an impresario's ''Who's Who'': Ernest Hemingway, Dorothy Parker, Pablo Picasso, Gertrude Stein, Alice B. Toklas and most significantly of all, F. Scott Fitzgerald and his mentally unstable wife, Zelda. If the villa ran out of rooms, they were sent up the road to the tiny Hotel du Cap, which the Murphys had persuaded the owner to keep open in the summer.

In Fitzgerald's novel *Tender is the Night*, Gerald and Sara Murphy are the original Dick and Nicole Diver in the chapters set in Antibes, where of the Divers, it is said, 'They have to like it. They invented it.'

The same might have been said of Frank Jay Gould, son of an American railway millionaire, whose hotel development at Juan-les-Pins virtually created the modern resort, which was ideal for summer visitors, but severely short of winter entertainment: a clear indication of the changing pattern.

The Americans liked the comforts of home that Gould and others provided in their hotels: en suite bathrooms, fresh soap (hitherto a commodity hoarded by French hoteliers), refrigeration and air conditioning. Sealed windows kept out mosquitoes, a serious problem in summer until DDT was first successfully used as an insecticide, in 1939. The French Frigidaire company cornered the market in compact fridges, demonstrating one at Nice in a mobile home as early as 1926.

All these advances in taste and technology removed the inconveniences of the summer climate, and left only the sea and the sun. Sunbathing and swimming were the order of the day at glamorous new swimming pools such as the Eden Roc Swimming Club, favoured haunt of Hollywood film stars and hangers-on. The major hotels acquired franchises for beaches directly opposite and turned them into microcosms of the hotel itself, with matching decor and prices. But less expensive hotels also began to be built, in response to new French laws that required companies to give holidays with pay. As a result, French families of much more modest means came to the Riviera for the first time, most of them in summer, and especially in August.

After the collapse of the Western Front in 1940, the hard-pressed British Government diverted two ancient colliers to Cannes to rescue its nationals. The French fleet, faced with the choice of being taken over by the Germans or the British, scuttled itself humiliatingly at Toulon. Under the terms of the armistice, the South of France retained an uneasy autonomy until November, 1942, when the Italians occupied the Riviera. They gave Monaco only their passing attention, and it proved the escape route of many Allied prisoners of war.

In August, 1944, a large American force invaded the South of France near Saint-Tropez, almost wrecking the town in a preliminary bombardment. Although Marseille, Toulon and Nice were taken in under three weeks, the Riviera was almost unrecognisable as a holiday resort.

Although it took years to repair the Riviera, almost as soon as the war ended, the rich returned. Some came by air: services to Nice from London began in June, 1948. However train travel retained its popularity, helped by the revival of the Blue Train, and the introduction of the Mistral, complete with four restaurant cars and a hair-dressing salon.

Although, in the end, these lavish trains proved uneconomic and were discontinued, it was not really because of competition in the air. The French government steadfastly refused to open the Riviera to the charter market that turned the Spanish and Italian coastline into mass tourist destinations. It did not need to: in the 1960s and 1970s the South of France enjoyed a boom period on a much higher threshold of expenditure. Enormous investment was made in new hotels, luxury apartment blocks, marinas, huge hypermarkets and motorways, which served to increase traffic rather than relieve it.

The agreeable climate could not in itself explain the attraction of the South of France, for much of the year over-populated and over-priced. It was fundamentally aspirational: of glamour, the good life and sexual freedom, epitomised by the bikini, first publicised in 1946 by Mario Brun, a gossip columnist for *Nice-Matin*, and worn by Martine Carol the following year at the first Cannes Film Festival.

The Riviera's agreeable climate encouraged the display of more minute (yet more expensive) items of swimwear year after year. It led inexorably to topless bathing and in many places total nudity, tolerated by the authorities, apart from one Keystone Cops raid on the beaches of Saint-Tropez. This quiet fishing village became the mecca of fashionable society after the French film producer Roger Vadim took his young wife there in 1956 to display her considerable charms in a film entitled *And God Created Woman*. It established an image of the Riviera that seems likely to endure long after Brigitte Bardot has passed into contemporary history. Perhaps Eve, fresh out of Paradise, could profitably have moved on farther west from Menton.

3
Food and Drink

Food

Whatever the modern reputation of Provence as a haven of gastronomy, washed down with fine wines, it has no origins in history. The high-born of the Court and the Church enjoyed a highly spiced and dangerously rich international cuisine; while the rank and file ate no better than their counterparts all over Europe, existing largely on soup and vegetables, or on pasta in those parts of Provence under Italian influence. In terms of tradition, therefore, Provençal specialities are little more than an ingenious work of propaganda by Frédéric Mistral in his efforts to revive what he saw as the true culture of the region. The vast majority of its inhabitants never saw from one day to the next the ingredients of the dishes on the great tables: they simply could not afford fruit, or meat, or fish, or even the olive oil for cooking.

With one exception: *bouillabaisse.* Until it became fashionable and expensive, *bouillabaisse* was a means by which fishermen and hostelries disposed of fish too scrawny to be served as part of a main meal. Now it has become the most famous dish of Provence, the speciality of Marseille, though almost ubiquitous to the coast of the Côte d'Azur. Even the experts disagree fundamentally on what the stew should contain, provided that the seasoning includes saffron and garlic. Its fish must be fresh, and should include the conger eel, red gurnet and especially the spiky hog-fish (*rascasse*). In some places, lobster is allowed; and in Toulon, the ingredients usually include potatoes, of which the purists thoroughly disapprove. A genuine *bouillabaisse* must always be ordered the previous day and in large quantities, enough for four to six persons at least. A genuine *bouillabaisse* is always served so that the fish, some of them pretty hideous in appearance, are separate from the stock.

There are many other Provençal fish specialities. The best, for some better than *bouillabaisse*, is *bourride*, a more straightforward stew made with almost any white fish whose key ingredient is its sauce of the great Provençal *aïoli*, a garlic mayonnaise. When pounded into a purée and served with cod, it becomes *brandade de morue*, especially delicious when accompanied by slices of truffle, the black mushroom of the Vaucluse. Sea bass (*loup de mer*) is at its best when grilled with fennel or cooked lightly in a white wine *fumet*. Red mullet sometimes comes both unfilleted and unscaled, definitely an acquired taste. *Ecrevisse*, or crayfish, are a superb delicacy served in a rich and extremely messy sauce.

Inland, the stews become largely meat-based, of beef, lamb or chicken, known as *daubes*, cooked in a broth of herbs and wine, using a *daubière*, a sealed casserole dish. *Agneau de Sisteron* is a lamb variation grilled on a wood fire. *Gardiane d'agneau* is a speciality of the Camargue, a lamb stew with olives, sometimes called *boeuf en daube* or *boeuf à la Gordienne*, when stewed in red wine.

The predominance of fresh vegetables in Provence explains why, alone of all the regions of France, a vegetable entrée is invariably served before the main course but after the *hors d'oeuvre*, of which the regional speciality is *tapenade*, a purée of oil, crushed olives and anchovies. Tomatoes *à la provençale* are a common offering, cut in half, covered in olive oil, parsley and garlic, then grilled. Asparagus is a particularly popular Provençal vegetable, as well as aubergines, cooked in a stew with peppers and tomatoes to make *ratatouille*. Artichokes are offered *à la Barigoule*, stuffed with garlic and parsley. Courgettes sometimes come as *tian de courgettes et tomatoes*, covered with Parmesan cheese and baked.

The *tian* is called after the durable terracotta dish used around Nice to create a much more substantial vegetable flan with eggs and a mixture of vegetables. Nice, for a long time an Italian city, also has its own version of pizza, *pissaladiera*, with anchovies, olives and cooked onions, and some local variants of pasta, not altogether successful. One of its specialities is *soupe au pistou*, a bean and courgette soup thickened with a paste of pounded basil, olive oil and garlic.

Another, *tourte aux blettes*, consists of an open-top pastry covered with leaves of chard, which taste rather like spinach. The city, however, has given its name to the famous *salade niçoise*, which should consist of hard-boiled eggs, quartered tomatoes, anchovies, olives, cucumber and spring onion.

Wine

Wine, Biblical miracles apart, is not made from water. Indeed water is one of the few non-injurious ingredients to be specifically prohibited, together with irrigation in the vineyards. If a drought results in smaller grapes than usual, and grapes with thick skins, then the owner of the vineyard can only hope for better things the following year. Provence, with its hostile sun-scorched climate, has never been the easiest of places in which to create memorable wines.

That said, the Rhône valley has been a natural wine-growing region since the days of the Greeks and the Romans, revived in the 14th century by the personal interest of the Avignon Popes. The classic wine of Provence is accordingly Châteauneuf-du-Pape, matured in small oak barrels for anything up to six years. The red — an inferior, rich, almost sweet white is also produced — is hugely expensive.

A few kilometres north-west, however, the village of Gigondas produces what many cognoscenti now claim to be an equally fine red wine, significantly cheaper, and much more readily available. It, too, has Appellation Contrôlée status, together with the sweet wines of nearby Beaumes-de-Venise, although they are usually drunk as an apéritif or to accompany the dessert. As with Châteauneuf-du-Pape and Gigondas, Beaumes has a less fashionable but equally palatable alternative, from the village of Rasteau, to the north-west.

Thereafter, outstanding Provence wines are few and far between. At la Palette, a tiny appellation hidden in the pine trees close to Aix-en-Provence, the single domain of Château Simone produces a distinctive rosé and an even better red. So does the Domaine de Trevallon, whose ripe and hugely palatable red is not allowed to join the Appellation Contrôlée recently bestowed on this wine-producing region, the Coteaux des Baux-en-Provence, because of its use of Cabernet Sauvignon grapes. The same fate has befallen the Mas de Daumas Gassac, which has produced an exceptional red within the otherwise mediocre region known as Vin de Pays de l'Herault.

Bandol, mainly produced on the stepped vineyards behind Toulon, is equally impressive as red, rosé or white wine, but the prices reflect the proximity of the Côte d'Azur. The estate with the best reputation for consistency across the full range of Bandol wines is Domaine de la Bastide Blanche.

Nearby Cassis, nothing to do with the blackcurrant liqueur, has perhaps the best white wines in Provence, fresh and fruity, and a high quality rosé. The leading estates are Clos Ste. Magdaleine and Domaine du Paternel.

As for Provence rosé, much is produced under the general appellation of Côtes de Provence and contributes more to a hangover than a tender palate. The best rosés are to be found on the extreme borders of the region, at Lirac, at Tavel, north-west of Avignon, certainly the supreme dry rosé,

and at Aigues-Mortes, where you can buy Listel *gris-de-gris*, the so-called wine of the sands, produced from vines growing by the sea.

Appropriately, perhaps, Provence has also provided arguably the greatest chef in the history of gastronomic cuisine, Auguste Escoffier (1846–1935), born at Villeneuve-Loubet, between Nice and Cannes. First at the Grand Hotel in Monte-Carlo, and later at the Savoy and Carlton in London, Escoffier formed a partnership with the hotelier César Ritz that made their establishments the talk of Europe. His recipes and cookery books form part of a fascinating gastronomic museum in his home town.

There are few genuine Provençal desserts, but two international favourites have their origin in Riviera folklore. Escoffier is said to have invented peach melba — peaches, ice cream, sugar and raspberry purée — for the singer Nellie Melba, while she was on tour in Monaco. A much younger and inexperienced sous-chef, Henri Charpentier, invented an equally famous dish by accident while learning the trade at the Paris Hotel in Monte Carlo. The Prince of Wales had come to dinner, and the nervous Charpentier accidentally set alight a pancake covered in curaçao and kirsch liqueur. The ravenous Prince nevertheless insisted on tasting the burnt dish, and found to general surprise that it had actually improved in flavour. Charpentier was asked its name, and on the spur of the moment said it was called 'Crêpe Princesse'. 'Why not call it Crêpe Suzette?' suggested the Prince, who was dining with a young actress of that name. So Crêpe Suzette it became.

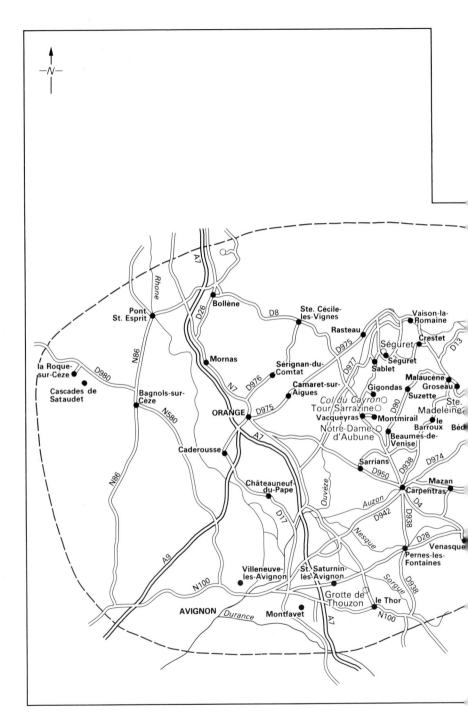

16

4
Avignon to Orange

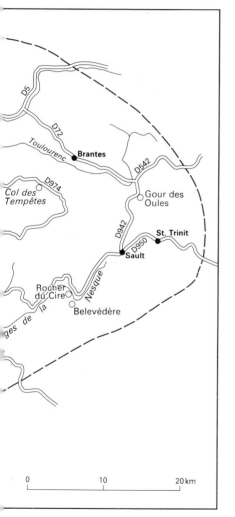

Some stuffy historians have poured scorn on the accuracy of the most famous nursery rhyme in France:

Sur le pont d'Avignon
L'on y danse, l'on y danse,
Sur le pont d'Avignon
L'on y danse tout'en ronde.

claiming that the bridge was too narrow for dancing in a ring, and that what dancing took place must have been underneath the bridge itself and in the shade of its arches — in other words, '*Sous le pont d'Avignon*'. But the rhyme was sung by children about children, and there was plenty of room on the bridge for small children to join hands and dance in a circle: especially after most of the bridge fell down and it became an ideal playground.

Le pont d'Avignon was always a sound commercial proposition, as Avignon lay at the confluence of the Rhône and the Durance, and the only bridge farther down the Rhône, at Arles, consisted simply of boats strung together. However it took the arrival of a young shepherd boy called Bénézet, who claimed to have seen the bridge in a vision, to provide the catalyst. Avignon merchants put up most of the money, local bishops the remainder, and in 1177 Bénézet was placed in holy orders and given the task of build-

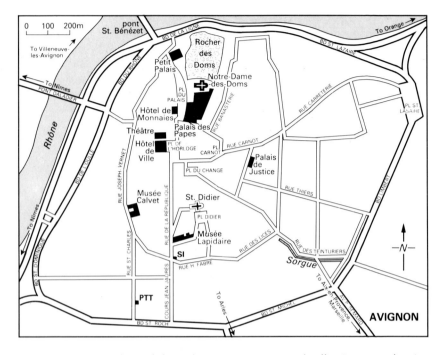

ing the bridge. He formed the volunteer labour force known as the Brotherhood of the Bridge, who completed the work by 1185. It had 22 arches, and stretched for more than 950yds. Bénézet was made a saint, the bridge bears his name, and Avignon was poised for the most dynamic period in its history.

In the 12th century Avignon, a tiny autonomous republic, ill-advisedly backed the Albigensian heretics (see page 74), and was absorbed into the Duchy of Provence. For supporting the crusade against the heretics, in 1274 the Papacy was given the Comtat Venaissin, whose boundaries were marked by the Rhône, the Durance, and Mount Ventoux.

The Comtat remained of little significance until the election in 1305 of the Archbishop of Bordeaux as Pope Clement V. He showed no signs of

wanting to rush off to Rome, as the city was close to anarchy. Against that, Clement had no wish to be obligated to the French King, Philip the Fair. His ingenious solution was to move the Papacy to the Comtat and himself into the Dominican convent in Avignon, by courtesy of the Duke of Provence.

Clement's successor from 1316 to 1334, John XXII, was already Bishop of Avignon, so he decided simply to enlarge the Bishop's Palace, on the great vantage point overlooking the Rhône, the Rocher des Doms, once a Ligurian and Roman stronghold. The next Pope, Benedict XII, demolished the old Bishop's Palace, and replaced it between 1338 and 1341 with a rather austere building modelled on his own Cistercian order. This forms the northern part of the Palace of the Popes, separated by the Great Courtyard from the spectacularly ornate additions of Clement VI to the west and south.

Clement, elected Pope in 1342, created a palace and Gothic fortress all in one, with huge machicolated square towers, some of them 150ft high. The thickness and height of the walls magnified the impression of towering menace. Together the two parts of the Palace extend over 15,000 sq m, and yet they were built in less than 20 years. By comparison the city walls look unimpressive: in the 14th century, however, they were surrounded by a deep moat, with 39 towers along a 5km circumference.

Under Clement Avignon at last became the legitimate property of the Popes. In 1347 Jeanne de Baux, Queen of Naples and Countess of Provence, rid herself of her objectionable husband, Andrew of Hungary, by having him strangled. Unfortunately from her point of view, Andrew's brother, Louis of Anjou, King of Hungary, organised an expedition to Italy to bring the Queen to account. Jeanne had to clear her name in the eyes of her nobles, and in 1348 she set out by galley for Avignon. Aged twenty, strikingly beautiful, she disembarked beneath the Pont St-Bénézet and with eight Italian cardinals in attendance, rode a magnificent white charger up to the Palace, her long tresses and blue mantle flowing in the breeze. Jeanne's proposition was simple: if the Pope absolved her from any complicity in the murder of her husband, he could buy Avignon for the derisory sum of 80,000 ducats. Assisted in his decision, it was maliciously alleged, by certain more personal favours, Clement VI sent her happily on her way.

The Palace of the Popes was stripped of its treasures during the French Revolution, and few of Clement's artistic acquisitions have survived. However, look out on the first floor for the five superb Gobelins tapestries in the Salle des Festins or Banqueting Hall, which could seat 150; leading off the Hall is St Martial's Chapel, with rich, dark-blue frescoes of the Saint c.1344 by Matteo Giovannetti, a contemporary of Giotto. Retracing one's steps slightly, at the end of this wing is the huge kitchen with a great chimney, and a waste system common to a sequence of stacked latrines, all dropping into a deep open ditch; slightly before the days of the public health inspector.

This so-called Latrine Tower was later also known as the Tour de la Glacière, or Ice House Tower. A month after Avignon threw in its lot with fanatics of the French Revolution, in October, 1791, about 60 Royalist men, women and children were cast dead and alive from here into an *oubliette*, a tiny windowless cell for prisoners whose normal fate was to be starved and forgotten. Their fate proved unimaginably worse: the cell was immediately filled with quicklime.

Beyond the Banqueting Hall is the tiny Papal Bedchamber, whose walls and ceilings are painted with hundreds of birds. The window embrasures have been designed to look like exotic birdcages with open doors, rather a nice touch. It leads into the first room in the New Palace, Pope Clement's study, called the Stag Room, after its woodland wall paintings (c.1343) beneath an ornate, larchwood ceiling.

At the end of the Papal apartments is the Clementine Chapel, which may look familiar to anyone who has visited Amiens Cathedral. Their ground

The Palace of the Popes and the Pont St. Bénézet, Avignon

measurements are identical, but not the height, because to avoid it becoming a target of siege weapons, the Chapel roof had to remain below the level of the ramparts. Its porch is lit by the Great Window of the Indulgence, where the pope would give his blessing to the crowds waiting in the Grand Courtyard below.

The Grand Staircase leads to the Great Audience Chamber, which was the seat of the Rota, so called because of its large circular table seating the Papal Tribunal that pronounced on all ecclesiastical matters. Appeals were held in the adjacent Lesser Audience Chamber, which is immediately beneath the Conclave Gallery, notable both for its elegant vaulted ceiling and for the fact that it led to the Conclave. The name is derived from a 13th-century

incident in Rome, when the Cardinals procrastinated for three years over a successor to Pope Clement IV, and the great families of Rome had them locked up *cum clave* until they reached a decision. In Avignon the Cardinals were literally walled in the Conclave: doors and windows were bricked up to a height of $7\frac{1}{2}$m. As an added refinement, their rations were reduced progressively each day until they elected a new Pope, which concentrated their minds wonderfully.

Rome eventually recovered the Papacy, though only after a bizarre period of rival Popes known as the Great Schism, which effectively ended in 1403 with the departure from Avignon of Benedict XIII to his native Spain. Losing the Popes made little difference to Avignon's prosperity, as until it was incorporated into France during the Revolution, a sequence of largely benevolent Papal Legates ruled the city. One of them, Cardinal Borghese, built his own residence (now called the Hotel des Monnaies) in front of the Palace of the Popes in 1616; later it became the Mint, then the Conservatory of Music. Borghese's family emblems, eagles and dragons, garnish the façade. Towards the Rhône, and close by the Pont St. Bénézet, stands the Petit Palais, rebuilt towards the end of the 15th century by Cardinal Giulio della Rovere, afterwards Pope Julius II. A great patron of the arts, he started the collection completed by a 19th-century Italian businessman, Campana di Cavelli. Its group of magnificent Italian primitives includes the 'Virgin Enthroned', painted in 1310. But the exhibition as a whole is remarkable, embracing the Siennese, Venetian and Florentine Schools, including the 'Virgin and Child' by Sandro Botticelli.

For another outstanding collection of pictures, visit the Musée Calvet in the Rue Joseph-Vernet, including, appropriately enough, works by Vernet himself, born in Avignon in 1714. It also contains an exceptional Italian landscape by Camille Corot and some classic views of Avignon and Fontaine-de-Vaucluse. Other notable exhibits include 15th century wrought-iron-work and 4th century BC Greek sculptures. The Museum was a private house in the 18th century, when its gardened courtyard is believed to have been the secret test ground of the Montgolfier brothers, who constructed the first practical balloon.

In an annexe of the Musée Calvet, the Lapidary Museum, once a Jesuit College, has two exceptional pieces of sculpture: 'Venus of Pourrières',

probably Roman, which has a curious incrustation caused by the clay in which it was buried; and 'Tarasque of Noves', a piece from the Second Iron Age showing a lion about to feast on two unfortunate Gauls. Only a street away, the Church of St. Didier (3rd-century origins; rebuilt 1335–1359), just off the rue de la République, has a 1478 Renaissance altarpiece in the first of its little chapels, by the Italian sculptor Francesco Laurana. It is known as 'Notre Dame de Spasme' because of the captivating look of anguish on the face of the Virgin as she watches Jesus struggling with the Cross.

A few minutes to the south-west, stroll along the cobbled rue des Teinturiers, which in English would no doubt be called 'Dyers Row'. It runs along a tributary of the river Sorgue, whose water was doubly useful as an ingredient of the dye and a means to turn the mill wheels that worked their machinery. A few of the wheels remain. As for the weavers, they had their own street, rue Banasterie, north-east of the Palace, full of grand houses and equally picturesque.

In the second half of July, the Grand Courtyard of the Palace is given over to performances in the annual International Drama Festival, when Avignon truly comes alive. Drumming up audiences almost overshadows what happens on the stage, as the actors, mainly students, compete for attention in a series of bizarre and often hilarious cameos around the streets. Most of the action takes place in the place de l'Horloge, called after the 14th–15th-century Clock Tower. Once the Roman Forum, the square is the centre of Avignon society, full of cafes and restaurants. The blank walls of nearby buildings have been animated by startlingly realistic decoration: painted people staring from painted windows. A huge two-tiered roundabout proves an irresistible magnet for children.

Children, too, will like the land train with open-sided carriages that runs from the place du Palais. It provides a 20-minute flavour of Old Avignon and also operates to the adjacent Rocher des Doms, whose raised garden offers a lovely view of the Pont St. Bénézet and the Rhône.

Below the Rock, the cathedral Notre-Dame des Doms is predominantly 12th-century Romanesque but with alterations from the 14th to the 17th centuries. It contains an interesting 12th-century bishop's throne in white marble, and a late Gothic monument to John XXII.

The land train apart, Avignon is best seen on foot: the best place to park is underneath the Palais des Papes, reached by way of the gate close to the Pont St Bénézet. The bridge itself has had an adventurous history. Badly damaged in 1226 during the Albigensian struggles, it was rebuilt and simultaneously raised between 1234 and 1237. The Romanesque Chapel of St. Nicolas on the second pier had to be adjusted to the height of the new bridge by adding a supplementary Gothic vault. Its original barrelled vault can still be seen in the Gothic chapel superimposed on the structure in 1513. Half the bridge collapsed during floods in 1668 and when a last attempt at repair was abandoned in 1680, only four of the original 22 arches remained.

Although for centuries the Rhône was the principal highway to Orange, in boats pulled upstream by teams of horses, struggling against the current, the most interesting route requires a wide loop via Carpentras and Vaison-la-Romaine. Head east from Avignon on N100 then north-east on D1 towards Pernes-les-Fontaines: there are many tempting diversions on the way. From the N100, you can detour south on N7F to **Montfavet** and its 14th-century Gothic church, originally part of a much grander monastery. Rejoin the N100 as far as **Le Thor**, whose charming church, predominantly Romanesque and 13th-century, has Gothic vaulting in the single aisle thought to be the first example of its kind in Provence. About 1.5 km to the north on D16, the **Thouzon Grotto** consists of underground caves with spectacular, needle-shaped stalactites.

Venasque, to the east, on the foothills of the Ventoux plateau, occupies a natural defensive position; a fortified village overlooking the river Nesque and once capital of the Comtat Venaissin (see page 18). Then, as now, it was a vast agricultural tract, irrigated by little streams, sheltered from the Mistral by a forest of cypress trees, with row upon row of grapes, strawberries, melons and tomatoes ripening under the hot spring sun.

Next to the Church of Notre Dame, notable primarily for its outstanding Crucifixion, a 1498 work of the Avignon School, is the so-called baptistery. Long thought to be an example of early Christian architecture, built under St. Siffrein in the 6th century, it has now been convincingly dated c1040. Near the bridge 3km north, the chapel Notre-Dame-de-Vie has a remarkable 7th-century Merovingian tombstone decorated with wheels and rosettes, commemorating Bishop Bohetius, who died in 604.

The village of **Mazan**, reached by skirting Carpentras east on D1, was once a garrison town on the Roman highway to Sault. The cemetery contains 62 Gallo–Roman sarcophagi, which originally lined that Roman road. They possess all the character of the sarcophagi at Alyscamps (see page 60), in much more serene surroundings.

Next to the cemetery stands the 12th-century chapel, Notre-Dame-de-Pareloup, literally, 'Our Lady Protectress against Wolves'. In those superstitious times, the villagers believed that vampires took on the appearance of wolves, dug up buried corpses and devoured them for their blood. Of course this can easily be explained away by the presence of hungry wolves in an area devoid of game. However, the church was also believed to be possessed, and fell into disuse and was left half-buried. Perhaps not the place to linger as the lengthening shadows signal the approach of night.

A notable detour from Mazan to the east is the dramatic D942 to Sault that runs the whole length of the **Gorges de la Nesque**. A precarious footpath winds down to the bottom of the Gorges from their highest point, a belvedere looking across to the Rocher du Cire, a sheer cliff 1,300ft high. Its literal meaning is the 'Rock of Wax', because generations of wild bees have nested in what can truly be called its tiny, honeycombed caves, coating the rock with wax.

Sault is perhaps the sweetest smelling place in all Provence, perfumed by great acres of lavender, at their peak in July, and prepared in local factories. Formerly Roman *Saltus*, only ruins of the 16th-century baronial castle remain in this tranquil market town.

To the north-east, 8km via D942

and D542, the **Gour des Oules** offers a dramatic excursion, a wild ravine overlooking the valley of the Toulourenc. Almost as desolate and eerie is the tiny village of **St. Trinit**, 7km on the D950, with a 12th-century Romanesque church, originally endowed by the Benedictine monks of Villeneuve-les-Avignon.

Ravaged by the Barbarians, which accounts for its ill-preserved Roman arch, **Carpentras** did not fully recover until the Avignon Popes made it the capital of the Comtat Venaissin. It was a favourite summer watering hole of the Cardinals, and of Pope Clement V (1305–1314), when it had outgrown its original city walls (marked by the present-day circular, tree-lined boulevards), so much so, that a second wall had to be built in the second half of the 14th century.

Carpentras's new-found affluence may have been due to the Popes, but little money was found for maintaining its own principal place of worship, as the original Romanesque Cathedral of St. Siffrein collapsed in 1400. Its Gothic replacement, in the heart of the Old Town, was started in 1405 and completed in 1519. In the Trésor are some much earlier relics, including the 'Saint Mors', said to be a piece of the hoof from Emperor Constantine's horse, shod with a nail from the original Cross. The former Cathedral's extrovert south porch, built between 1470 and 1480, incorporates on the south gable the 'Boule Aux Rats', a globe gnawed by rats, whose origin is a mystery.

In the 14th century the Jews, persecuted in France, fled to the relative safety of the Comtat Venaissin. Their synagogue in Carpentras, in existence by 1367, was rebuilt between 1741

23

Nôtre Dame D'Aubune, Romanesque chapel at Beaumes-de-Venise (see p. 30)

and 1743 in sumptuous rococo style. It has ritual purification baths for men and women, called in Provençal the *cabussadou*, the 'head first'.

The Inguimbertine Library contains the personal collection of Malachie d'Inguimbert, who became Bishop in his home town in 1735. Bequeathed to the municipality on his death, it has nearly 230,000 works, including autographed scores by three great composers, Johann Sebastian Bach, Johannes Brahms and Robert Schumann. The library is located off boulevard Albin-Durand in the Musée des Beaux-Arts, housed in the Hotel d'Allemand, a splendid 18th-century mansion.

D'Inguimbert also founded a hospital in the magnificent Hôtel-Dieu,

erected between 1750 and 1752. Its outstanding features are the upper balustrades and the imposing ornamental staircase. Although still a hospital, visits are permitted to the Baroque chapel and the pharmacy, which has superb Italian faience inside panelled cupboards decorated with monkeys and surrealistic landscapes.

Modern Carpentras has been transformed by the creation of a pedestrian precinct in the old town, centred on the former cathedral. It is however a hectic agricultural centre, chaotic on Fridays, when a huge general market attracts shoppers from many kilometres around. This is the place to buy lavender water, truffles and *berlingots*, caramel sweets that are a Carpentras speciality.

From Carpentras, the D938 to Vaison-la-Romaine passes through **Le Barrou**, a village dominated by its huge Renaissance château, dating back to the 12th century and once a stronghold of the Lords of Les Baux (see page 54). The view from its terrace is remarkable. In summer, the village stages a fruit market distinguished for its *abricots roses*, pink apricots. A detour, via D19 on the right, skirts the southern slopes of Mont Ventoux (see page 25). Three kilometres short of Bedoin, the 11thC **Chapel of Sainte-Madeleine** is an exquisite example of Romanesque Provençal style. It has a huge square belfry and three small apsidal chapels covered by Provençal tiles. **Bedoin** itself is a delightful wine-growing village with ochre roofs and tiny squares. Its 17th-century church, built in Jesuit style, has an exceptional 18th-century altarpiece believed to have been the work of Pierre Mignard.

Few villages can claim to have a church founded by Charlemagne:

fewer still to have had it pulled down by a Pope, Clement V. Between 1309 and 1314 Clement, one of the Avignon Popes, had a summer residence, long disappeared, at Groseau, 2km from **Malaucène** on the D974. Concerned about his personal safety, Clement replaced the Romanesque church at Malaucène with little short of a fortress, somewhere he could retreat to in times of danger. The result is an unlikely looking 14th-century church whose round-arched windows of the nave are set at second storey height; above them are walls containing embrasures, with rectangular panels that resemble walled-up windows; and the west portal is protected by substantial machicolations.

Malaucène itself is a charming village, its narrow streets lined by plane trees. Its rather curious name means 'bad sands', a reference to the unstable ground on which many of the houses were built.

Malaucène's other claim to fame is as the starting point of Petrarch's famous climb of Mount Ventoux, at 1909m the tallest mountain in France between the Alps and the Pyrenees. It has been suggested that Petrarch invented his feat, but he left so detailed an account that it could only have come from direct experience. On May 9, 1336, accompanied by his brother and two servants, he left Malaucène at sunrise on an exhilaratingly clear day, and drank so deeply of the scenery at the summit that the party returned to Malaucène long after dark. From Groseau, the path that Petrarch took still leads to the top, but it is a particularly demanding climb, and dangerous in bad weather. Not for nothing is Mount Ventoux derived from the Provençal *Mont Ventour*, or 'windy

mountain'. Its white upper escarpments consist mainly of smooth limestone rock, totally devoid of vegetation, giving a snow-capped appearance even when all the snow has disappeared at the height of summer. By road, the D974 from Malaucène winds its way some 15km to the aptly named Col des Tempêtes, the 'pass of storms'. Although the view, and the ambience, are spoilt by the presence of an observatory, radar station and television transmitter, on a fine day Marseille is clearly in sight and sometimes even Mount Canigou in the eastern Pyrenees.

An equally spectacular road around the east face of Mont Ventoux reaches the tiny village of **Brantes**, with a permanent population of barely 100. Built on the steep north side of the Toulourenc valley, it seems almost on the point of slipping down the hillside. The ascent of Mont Ventoux by the east face begins at Brantes, where hikers can refresh themselves in summer with a *tisane*, made from local lime blossom, in the village cafe.

The eastern slopes of the Dentelles de Montmirail (see page 28 below) can be explored by leaving the D938 en route to Vaison-la-Romaine. **Suzette**, west of Malaucène on D90, is an isolated, sombre hamlet standing among stepped vineyards in a rocky landscape. **Crestet**, on D76, has a quaint, almost Lilliputian atmosphere, with the tiniest of squares, complete with 12th-century church and fountain; and narrow cobbled streets leading to a partially restored 11th-century castle, whose owner does not encourage visitors.

The river Ouvèze flows through **Vaison-la-Romaine**, a modern Provençal town, a medieval stronghold and a

Statue of Sabina, wife of Emperor Hadrian, Vaison-la-Romaine

sophistication of the Roman city. Beyond rue Burrin, the Puymin Quarter has lavish villas, notably the House of Messius, complete with bathroom suite. Other houses were built specifically to let. The *nyphaeum*, a central water cistern, distributed water to all parts of the town. A large municipal building embracing a garden, known as Pompey's Portico, benefited from sponsorship: the cost was underwritten by the Pompeia family. A tunnel through the hill leads to the theatre, cut into the natural slope, as they were in ancient Greece. Built cAD20, in the reign of Tiberius, it has the dramatic backdrop of the hillside and Mount Ventoux. In all 34 rows of seats rise up from the surviving columns of the portico. You can visit the pits used to store the theatre machinery, by which in certain productions, figures could rise dramatically as though from Hades. Beyond place Abbe Sautel to the south–west, the Quartier de la Villasse has a covered shopping precinct, pavements and gutters, and a communal five-seater latrine. Each little shop was in fact the front room of the terraced houses bordering the street, modest in comparison with the magnificent House of the Silver Bust, owned by a noble patrician whose silver bust once stood in the hallway of his property. It can now be seen in the museum in the Puymin Quarter, together with a white marble head of Venus, a statue of Tiberius, and two great statues, more than lifesize, of the Emperor Hadrian and the Empress Sabina.

Vasio, known as *urbs opulentissima*, richest city of them all, was destroyed by the Franks towards the end of the 5th century. The former cathedral of Notre-Dame de Nazareth, on the

Roman city all in one. Yet the richness of its treasures only became apparent after 1907, when an amateur archaeologist and local priest, Abbé Joseph Sautel, discovered fragments of the amphitheatre. Soon excavations revealed the full extent of the Roman remains covered by the river's alluvial soil, the long lost evidence of the city of *Vasio* listed in the 2nd century BC as part of the province of Gallia Narbonensis, which stretched across much of southern France.

North of the Roman bridge over the Ouvèze, 56ft and a single span, two separate areas of excavation reveal the

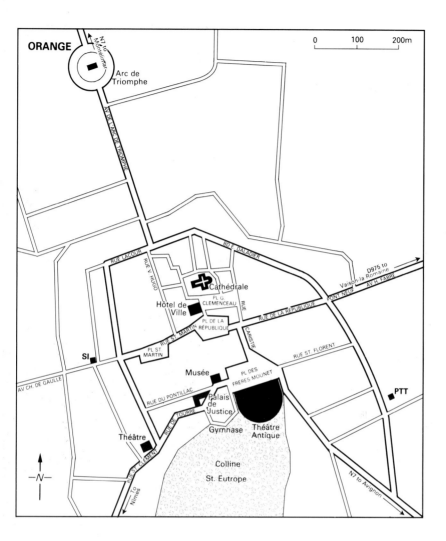

Roman side of the Ouvèze, dates from no earlier than the 10th century, though it stands on the foundations of an earlier Roman edifice of mysterious purpose. In the north apse, with its arcading supported on Romanesque columns, is a striking early Christian altar, decorated in relief.

Vaison, an early Christian bishopric, was captured by Raymond VI of Toulouse in 1160. Compelled to with-

draw by the Holy Roman Emperor, in 1193 the Counts built a castle on the rocky slope on the left bank of the Ouvèze, leaving the original town in ruins. As they must have expected, most of the inhabitants decided to put themselves under the protection of the castle. Finally even the bishop had to move closer to his flock, and Bishop Pons de Sade — another of the ubiquitous de Sade family whose history is an integral part of Provence — built a new cathedral in rue Principale of the Upper Town in 1464. By the 19th century the inhabitants felt little purpose was served in living in such an unhealthy and confined space on the hill, and they moved back down to the plain, building beyond the Roman ruins. In this unique way both Roman and medieval Vaison have survived without the layers of construction work that frustrate much archaeological investigation. The medieval town has become a fashionable summer resort, and many houses have been restored. The ruined castle is unsafe, and closed, but the climb is still worthwhile for the view of Mount Ventoux.

The **Dentelles de Montmirail** are the fabulous foothills of the Ventoux Range, forced upright by great convulsions in the mists of time and honed, as on some giant's lathe, by the wind and the weather. So delicate is this limestone mosaic that it has become the Dentelles, literally, lace points, only 375m at its highest point, though it seems much more. As for Montmirail, it survives as a tiny hamlet (see Vacqueras, page 30, below). A series of twisting roads encircles the Dentelles and links Vaison-la-Romaine with Malaucène and Beaumes-de-Venise, by way of some remote and picturesque villages. **Séguret**, 10km from Vaison on D977 and D98, built against the rock face, with cobbled streets and a ruined castle, is an artists' paradise in summer. For those who prefer a camera to a brush, the St.-Denis Church and the fortified Porte Reynier, both 12th-century, and the 15th-century Mascarons Fountain make a delightful foreground to views over the

The Roman theatre at Orange

Dentelles and the vineyards in the valley of the Rhône. **Sablet**, 2km on D23, has curious streets that run in concentric rings around an appealing hillock, and a crumbling 12th-century church. **Gigondas**, a further 5km via D7 and D79, is second only to Châteauneuf-du-Pape (see page 14) in producing an excellent red wine that can be tasted in a host of cellars around the main square. Its ruined castle is a relic from the days when the House of Orange owned this isolated principality.

Vacqueyras, on D7, once a Moorish stronghold, also has castle ruins and supporting fortifications. Close by are Montmirail, the Saracens' Cemetery and, to the north, the **Tour Sarrazine**, a 3rd-century ruined watchtower.

The Romanesque Chapel of **Notre-Dame-d'Aubune** is reached from D7 on a steep grass track. It may be difficult to believe this now, but the great trade road of the Greeks from Lyons to Massalia passed within a few hundred yards of this chapel, whose exceptional bell-tower is ornamented by tall, graceful pilasters and has survived almost intact. Much of the chapel was badly damaged during the Wars of Religion and for some years was used by marauding bands as a convenient whorehouse. The key is kept at the nearby Fontenouilles Farm.

Beaumes-de-Venise, 8km on D7 and D90, owes its name to the Venaissin in Comtat Venaissin (see pages 6–7), when its castle, now a ruin, was a strategic defensive point. The village is famous for its muscat wine. Southwest on D55, the church at **Sarrians** is a former Benedictine priory and stands close to another ruined Moorish tower.

Vaison-la-Romaine is linked to **Orange** by the Princes of Orange Road (D975) over which the rulers of Orange-Nassau travelled to their domains in Germany. First stop on the Princes of Orange Road is **Camaret-sur-Aigues**, a village whose fortified gates survive. The splendid Porte de l'Horloge, supported by two round towers, was provided with a wrought-iron belfry c1750.

In Orange itself, for over 2,000 years, the huge commemorative arch stood across the much more significant road to Rome. Founded as Arausio in 36BC by veterans of the Second Legion, it had a splendid temple, a vast sports stadium, baths, an amphitheatre, and the two great edifices that have survived to this day, the arch and the unique theatre.

When, in 1229, the Comtat Venaissin (see page 18) was given to the Pope, the Seigneurie of Orange was excluded: an enclave within an enclave. It eventually passed through marriage to William the Silent (1533–84), founder of the Dutch Republic, whose son, Maurice of Nassau, fortified Orange in 1622 by using the Roman remains and united the Principality with the Netherlands. Orange was finally ceded to France by the Treaty of Utrecht in 1713. It has since given its name to a religious sect in Ireland, a town in New Jersey and a district of California, a river and the Orange Free State in South Africa. Ironically, only oranges, a fruit introduced to Provence by the Moors, have positively no connection with the town of Orange.

The Roman theatre survives principally because Maurice of Nassau incorporated it into his city wall. Although, like the theatre at Arles, it was used as a stone quarry, it is the only Roman theatre in Europe whose façade remains intact. The theatre measures 104m in length and 38m in height, with seats, cut out of the hill, for as many as 40,000 spectators, though only sufficient for 10,000 have survived.

The infrastructure of elaborate scene-shifting equipment remains in place. The theatre is also unique in the survival of the square stone blocks which carried the masts supporting a series of triangular awnings that kept rain and sun off the auditorium. In the middle of the interior stage wall, a 3½m statue, probably of Augustus, has been painstakingly reassembled out of tiny fragments. A Barbarian pays him homage at his feet. Steps from the theatre lead to the excavations of an enormous Roman gymnasium or sports stadium, 457m long, complete with baths and steamrooms.

The commemorative arch, built between 26 and 1BC was converted into a fort with a crenellated tower by Raymond des Baux. Battlements and loopholes were later added. Despite this, it remains the best preserved Roman arch in France, with remarkable, rich motifs on every side. It is thought to commemorate Caesar's victories over the Gauls on land and the Greeks at sea. The naval triumph, embellished by anchors, ropes and the prows of ships, is an extremely rare example of recognition of success at sea by what was essentially a land-based military machine.

North of Orange, **Serignan-du-Comtat**, 10km on D976, in former papal lands, has the ruins of a castle belonging to the beautiful Diane de Poitiers (1499–1566), when she was the wife (from age 13) of Louis de Brèze, who left her a widow at 32. Diane became the mistress of Henry II of France, who in 1547 gave her the great Château of Chenonceau.

The French entomologist, Jean Henri Fabre (1823–1915), bought a house here in 1879 after the publication in Orange of the first volume of his *Souvenirs entomologiques* brought him immediate fame as the 'Insects' Homer'. It must have been a welcome reversal of fortune for Fabre, who in 1865 had been forced to resign his college post in Avignon and live almost in penury, because he had dared to teach female students the principle of the fertilization of flowering plants. His house, which he called l'Harmas, after the Provençal word for land in its natural state, stands on the outskirts of the village. It is now a museum, preserving his original study, his drawings, his specimens, and even the bag in which he collected insects out in the field.

The D976 continues to **St.-Cécile-les-Vignes**, once a Calvinist stronghold, and as the name might suggest, the centre of a wine-growing district. **Mornas**, 9km from Orange on N7, was initially a fortified village; but only the gates and a ruined castle remain of its original defences at the foot of a high cliff. Farther north D26 off N7 leads to **Bollène**, once the property of the popes. It was here that the celebrated professor of chemistry, Louis Pasteur (1822–95), showed that by inoculating pigs with swine fever, he could prevent their subsequently contracting the disease.

Just 5km north, via D160 and D218a, lies **Barry**, a prehistoric troglodytic settlement and medieval village built into the rocky hillside, overlooked by a 12th-century ruined castle. Completely overgrown and deserted, it

Gateway to Gaul: the Roman Arch of Tiberius at Orange

was last inhabited by the Albigensian religious sect. In ·1228 they were attacked by the Catholics, put to the sword, and their houses demolished.

On the western side of the N7, by D994, is **Pont-St.-Esprit**, literally Holy Spirit Bridge. Started in 1265, the bridge took 44 years to complete; it stretches 1,000m, and is slightly curved to resist the pressures of the current. A marvellous medieval panorama of riverside houses greets the visitors that cross the bridge, just as it must have done to foot-weary pilgrims, long ago. There are two outstanding detours from Pont-St.-Esprit. **L'Aven d'Orgac**, north on N86 then west on D901 and D174, consists of a series of great caverns discovered by Robert de Joly, head of the French Speleological Society, in 1935. In rather macabre

fashion, an urn containing his heart has been embedded in one of the vast stalagmites that make these caves such a breathtaking spectacle. The largest is vast, 255m long and up to 140m in height; three in all can be seen to a depth of 185m, where the temperature is about 12°C, so take a light sweater in summer. The caves are quite safe for the old and the young, provided that they can navigate the 788 steps down and, especially, up.

La Roque-sur-Cèze, south–west on D23, D166, is a delightful hilltop village spiralling upwards from its Roman-esque chapel, with a ruined citadel above and the river Cèze below, spanned by a multi-arched medieval bridge with sharply-pointed piers. The river seems tranquil here, but half a mile downstream it plunges over the

Cascade du Sataudet, a swirling spectacular torrent between the limestone rocks.

Just south of Orange on D17, **Calderousse** has a notable 16th-century chapel, lying in the watershed of the river Rhône. It was protected by a dyke whose gates in medieval times were made water-tight by applying great wads of cow dung to the cracks. **Châteauneuf-du-Pape**, on D68, was the summer residence of John XXII (1244–1334), one of the Avignon popes, who started work on his château in 1317. The château was burnt down in the 16th century and though its great keep survived, most of it was blown up by the German Army during their retreat in 1944. Pope John and his predecessor, Clement V (1305–1314) encouraged the planting of vines, part of an ecclesiastical tradition, that had declined over the centuries. Châteauneuf-du-Pape was an ideal location, where an old course of the Rhône had left a sea of smooth pebbles that reflected the sun's rays on to the ripening grapes. In 1923 the Baron Le Roy won a legal battle that allowed only local producers to sell their wine as Châteauneuf-du-Pape, the forerunner of the Appellation Contrôlée system of today.

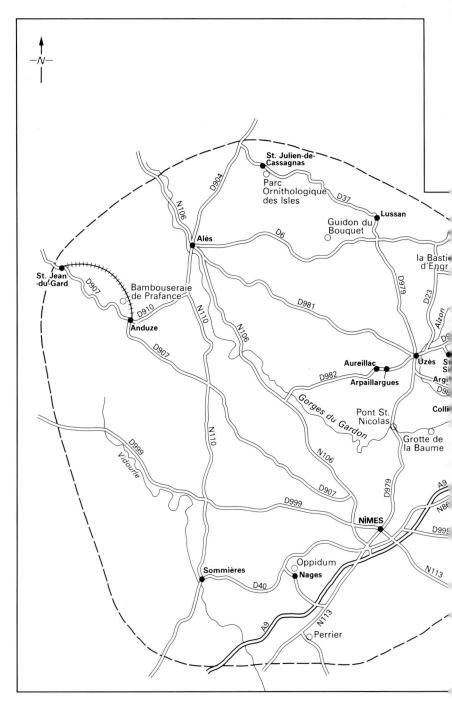

5
Avignon to Nîmes

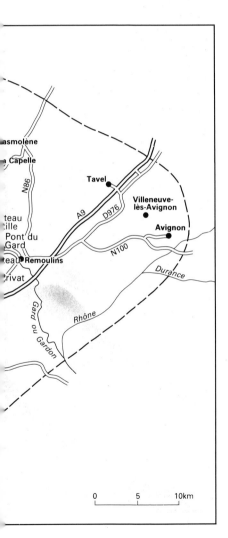

Leave Avignon westwards on N100 by **Villeneuve-lès-Avignon**, literally, 'new town near Avignon', perhaps the first example of commuters forced out by rising prices in the city centre. Certainly the cardinals were unable to find suitable accommodation in Avignon to live in style, so in the 14th century they put up their palatial houses at the other end of the Pont St.-Bénézet. At one stage there were at least fifteen magnificent residences, known as *livrées*, and Villeneuve kept its exclusivity even after the loss of the bridge. However most the big houses were destroyed during the Revolution, and only three remain.

The Cardinals enjoyed the protection of the King of France, Philippe the Fair, who fortified the Villeneuve end of the bridge with a tower that bears his name. This extremely strong fortification, with its foundations embedded in the rock, took 14 years to complete (1293–1307), because of intervening wars. Later in the 14th century a third storey was added, then a watchtower. The surviving terrace, for those able to climb 176 steps, gives a good idea of the tower's strategic value, as it commands remarkable views over the Rhône and Avignon; the silhouette of the Palace of the Popes at sunset is a memorable sight.

St. André fort, originally on an island

St. André's fort: once the gateway to Avignon

in the Rhône, with its single fortified gate dominated by twin rotund towers, is a classic example of medieval military architecture. Visitors can see the bread oven, carefully marked out to ensure even rations, presumably in time of siege; and the graffiti left in the dungeon by the prisoners.

Midway between the tower and the fort, is the Church of Notre Dame, founded in 1333 by Cardinal Arnaud de Via, the autocratic nephew of Pope John XXII. Its 15th-century sacristy contains a beautifully shaped 14th-century image of the Virgin, in polychrome ivory.

Behind the fort, and once on the bank of the Rhône, the Charterhouse of Val de Benediction, founded in 1356, was once the largest in France. In all it covers six acres, and resembles a small village with streets, cottages and cloisters. Its chapel contains some beautiful frescoes by Viterbo. At its heyday it housed hundreds of monks from the Carthusian order, which forbade conversation except on Sundays. The monks were expelled

Genius of Roman engineering: le Pont du Gard

Pont du Gard

Spanning the sylvan banks of the river Gardon for more than 2,000 years, the Pont du Gard is a supreme testimony to Roman imagination and power. It was built by Marcus Agrippa, son-in-law of the Emperor Augustus, about 19BC as part of a prodigious scheme to carry water 40km miles from the river Eure to the rising Roman city of *Nemausus*, modern-day Nîmes.

The Pont du Gard, 274m long, 50m high, consists of three tiers of arches: six crossing the river; eleven wider, lighter arches above; and finally 35 small arches that accommodated the water duct in a covered canal. Each span of the aqueduct varies slightly in width, enhancing its harmonious perspective; and each arch was built independently, to reduce the risk from subsidence. The piers were constructed on semi-circular wooden frames, each huge stone winched up into place by gangs of slaves, using a block and tackle harnessed to a line of goats. The ochre coloured stones, some of them weighing as much as 6 tonnes, were laid entirely without cement or mortar: the courses simply held together by iron clamps.

The weakness of the entire Gard aqueduct was its vulnerability to sabotage. The first hint that Nemausus was about to be attacked often came from the interruption to its auxiliary water supply, in peaceful times enough to provide an average of 400 litres per citizen per day. After the 4th century, however, the channel progressively silted up with lime deposits, until in the 9th century it became blocked and fell into disuse. Its stones were pilfered for other construction, and in the 16th century some of lighter arches were partially cut away to allow pack horses to cross. However in the 19th century Napoléon III spent lavishly on its reconstruction.

In summer, when traffic at the bridge can be chaotic, a one-way system operates, so to drive alongside the aqueduct, follow the signs for 'Rive Gauche' from Remoulins. Use the car park just short of the bridge, as it is less vulnerable to thieves.

For the best view of the superstructure, especially for afternoon photography, from the main road walk under the Pont du Gard upstream on the right bank for about 135m, near the entrance to the Château de St-Privat. There are several convenient places for picnics or bathing. From close by the Château, a narrow path winds up to the eastern end of the upper tier of the Pont du Gard. It can be crossed on foot, but on the very top only by those with a good head for heights, as there is nothing between you and the dizzy drop into the river below.

during the Revolution and the Charterhouse fell into disrepair, but it has been gradually restored. It is now a centre for scientific and cultural seminars.

Much of the monks' property found its way into the Municipal Museum, including chests and cupboards, but its great treasure is the '*Coronation of the Virgin*'. It was painted in 1453 by Enguerrand Charonton (or Quarton) for the Abbot of the Charterhouse, Abbé de Montagnac, in 1453.

N100 leads to **Remoulins**, whose medieval wall and Romanesque church are overshadowed by the nearby Pont du Gard (see box).

Then head north–west to **Argilliers**, a village dominated by its neo-Classical 16th-century Château Castille, largely reconstructed by the Baron de Castille during the 18th century. Although the interior is closed, the exterior is superb, set off to perfection by an avenue of yew trees leading to a balustered peristyle in front of the Château. Its columns and balustrades are surrounded by an extensive colonnade.

Continue north–west for an extended visit to the entrancing medieval town of **Uzès**, perhaps after a brief detour left to visit the picturesque hamlet of **Collias**, on the Gardon river. Built on a hill overlooking the Alzon valley, Uzès is supremely picturesque, a tiny Duchy with narrow, arcaded streets and towers reminiscent of San Gimignano, near Siena. Indeed there is evidence that Uzès was influenced far more than Provence proper by Italian style, as its 12th-century Fenestrelle Tower is unique in France but relatively common in northern Italy. It was once part of the Romanesque St. Théodorit's Cathedral, destroyed during the Wars of Religion. Its six stories, with abundant windows (hence its name), rise 138ft from a square foundation through ingeniously reducing circular stages, to end in a low pyramidal roof.

Some of the other surviving towers can be seen from a single narrow street off the main square, the Rue Entre-les-Tours. The Tour du Roi is mainly 12th-century, so, directly opposite, is the square Tour des Evêques, now the Clock Tower. The Bermonde, built by an 11th-century nobleman, once dominated the countryside; the view from the top is worth the climb up 148 steps. From the balustrade of the Bermonde, added in 1839, you can see into the courtyard of the Ducal

Not quite Pisa: the Fenestrelle tower at Uzès

Palace, which contains two towers, one a 16th-century Gothic chapel (with restoration from the 19th century) with tombs of the ducal family, the other a 14th-century octagonal turret. Known as the Vicomte, the Palace was built to celebrate the elevation of the Uzès family to a viscounty in 1328. The Renaissance façade was designed by Philibert Delorme, who built the Tuileries in Paris.

As the Uzès family still lives in the palace, only part of it is open to the public, notably the Grand Salon from the Louis XVI period with contemporary furniture and costumes.

In 1632 Louis XIII gave Uzès the honorary title of 'the premier Duchy of France'. The town, however, was a Huguenot stronghold, which led

Richelieu to demolish its considerable ramparts, now replaced by a circular boulevard. No longer of strategic significance, Uzès entered a new era of prosperity as a linen and silk centre.

Place aux Herbes, strictly place de la République, recently restored, has a striking façade of fine noble houses, shaded by plane trees and overlooking a fountain. The town market and many country fairs are held in the square.

Between the square and the Palace, note the Hôtel Joubert et d'Avejan with its fine 16th-century façade; and the Hôtel Dampmartin, also 16th-century, with Renaissance façade and inner courtyard. The Hôtel de Ville stands opposite the castle gateway: it dates from Louis XVI, and was erected in 1773. The road from the Palace leads past the former Mint, a reminder of the era when bishops could strike their own coins, to the 17th-century former Bishop's Palace. On the far side of the square is the Hotel Baron de Castille, late 18th-century, complete with impressive colonnade.

St. Théodorit Cathedral contains an exceptional gilded organ, dating back to the 17th century, with 18th-century pipes. It stands between the Bishop's Palace and the Promenade des Marroniers, a wide shaded avenue lined with chestnut trees and over-looking the *garrigue* or park of the dukes. At the end of the avenue, the Racine Pavilion commemorates the brief stay in 1861 of Jean Racine, the great classical dramatist. Unfortunately Racine was less captivated by Uzès, which he believed broadened its bodies but not its minds:

Adieu, ville d'Uzès, ville de bonne chère,
Ou vivraient vingt traiteurs, ou mourrait un libraire.

Which could be translated in contemporary fashion:

Farewell to Uzès, whose library is replaced
By twenty take-aways: a singular disgrace.

East of Uzès is a cluster of castles. First visit **St.-Siffret**, by D982 and D404, a perched village whose ruined castle was built by the Templars. D23, then D211, on the right, leads to the medieval castle of **la Bastide d'Engras**. Or stay on D982, turn left on D219, to see the ruined castles at **la Capelle** and **Masmolène**, a pair of attractive villages.

North–west of Uzès, the D979 passes through **Lussan**, a fascinating perched village with views of the Garrigues peaks (see below). Detour off the D979 by D6 and D607 to the **Guidon du Bouquet**, a beak-shaped rock (1,998ft), with fine views. Rather farther, some 32km in all from Uzès via D979, D37 and D132, about 1km south-east of **St. Julien-de-Cassagnas**, is the Parc Ornithologique des Isles with its collection of 1,000 exotic birds.

South of Uzès lies a limestone plateau covered in vivid wild foliage and hollowed out by ancient rivers into fierce gorges. Known as the Garrigues, it was a refuge for the Protestants during the religious wars.

The Pont St.-Nicholas, a 13th-century bridge of seven arches, spans the Gardon river in a delightful location. It was built by The Brother-hood of the Bridge, who did not rest on their achievement at Avignon (see page 18), but spanned other rivers, too. Just beyond the bridge, there are further spectacular views of the Gardon Gorge. A rapidly deteriorating road leads to the Gorge itself by way of a compulsory car park, from where the

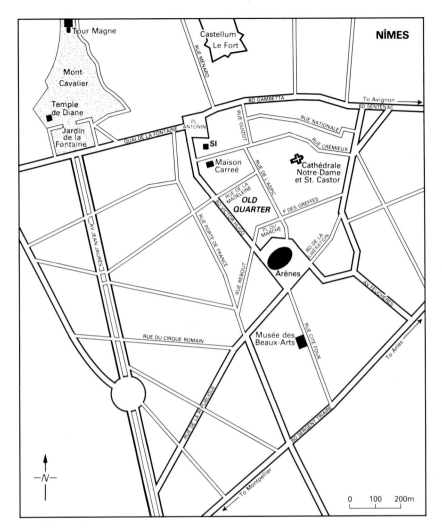

Gorge is a further 30 minutes away on foot. Also worth a visit is the **Grotte de la Baume**, reached from a cliff in the far bank of the River Gardon. Return to the D979 and head south to Nîmes.

A sprawling industrial complex, **Nîmes** is best visited on a Sunday or public holiday, when the approach roads are not congested with commercial traffic. Even on the busiest days, however, the effort is worthwhile to see the great monuments to Roman power, the amphitheatre and the temple.

Nîmes began as Nemausus, named after the god of the spring that gushes out of the rock at the foot of the city's hill, Mount Cavalier. In the last century BC it acquired some importance at the end of the Roman Civil War as a home for retired soldiers of the legions, when it was fortified by Emperor Augustus.

The great Roman amphitheatre

dates back to CAD50, probably built by the architect Crispius Reburrus, also responsible for the amphitheatre at Arles (see page 57). Arles is slightly larger, but the Nîmes arena is the best preserved in the Roman world. Measuring 101m by 133m, and 21m in height, it ranks twentieth in size of the 70 surviving amphitheatres. Unlike the Arles arena, its attic level has survived, where the slaves sat until it was time to organise their masters' transport home. The two superimposed stories of 60 arches carry 34 rows of seats, with room for between 21,000 and 24,000 spectators. Yet the circular, barrel vaulted galleries and 124 exits are so cleverly arranged that the entire stadium could be evacuated in under five minutes.

Huge awnings protected the spectators from the afternoon sun. The actual arena was watertight, ready to be flooded for sea battles with water carried over the Pont du Gard. Chariot races were staged despite the tight turns. However gladiators, kept in underground cells until they were summoned for battle, provided the principal fare. Wild animals were almost certainly never used in this amphitheatre, as the retaining wall is too low to have confined an athletic lion. However that does not deter the Nîmois from staging Spanish and the slightly less bloody Provençal-style bullfights in the arena, when the addition of modern seating tends to spoil the effect.

The amphitheatre survived because it was more useful as an entity than as a source of raw materials. The Visigoths turned it into a fortress, digging a deep moat, blocking three of the four exits, and constructing towers inside the walls. In the 11th century it was the headquarters of a band of zealous young nobles, the *Milites Castri Arenarium*, the Knights of the Arena; they lived on its east side, behind three walled-up arcades pierced by tiny windows.

After Nîmes became part of the Kingdom of France in 1227, the amphitheatre became a city within a city, accommodating more than 2,000 people crowded together in 150 tiny houses. A church was built in the centre, dedicated to St. Martin, the soldier-saint. When the area was finally cleared in 1809, after the French Revolution, rubble and rubbish 8m deep had to be removed before the floor of the arena was reached.

Less than 1km to the north, the masterpiece of Roman architecture, the Maison Carrée, is the best preserved Roman temple still in existence. Like the Pont du Gard, it was probably built by Marcus Agrippa; it was certainly dedicated to his two sons, Caius and Lucius.

The temple was possibly consecrated to the three gods known as the Captoline Trinity, Juno, Jupiter and Minerva, because it was known locally as the Capitol until the 16th century. It then became the Maison Carrée, or Square House, a curious description, as it is far from square. Standing on a huge podium, it measures 25m by 12m, with a deep porch of three bays and engaged Ionic columns down the sides and rear of the cella, or inner sanctum. The steps to the temple are restricted to the entrance façade, which has a lavishly decorated entablature. To describe it as having a strong Greek influence is to understate its importance, as it is as magnificent as any Greek original.

The Maison Carrée also survived

Jeans and Tobacco

By the early 1700s, when peaceful times at last prevailed, Nîmes became a centre of the silk and woollen industries. A rough twilled overall was first made in Nîmes for the common workman in the 19th century, and successfully exported. Each overall was marked 'de Nîmes', to indicate its place of manufacture: it was soon contracted to 'denim', which eventually came to mean the cloth itself. Levi Strauss is believed to have asked Nîmes to supply another durable cloth, with which he made his first, famous blue jeans.

Apart from denim, Nîmes has also contributed another word to the language. It was the birthplace of Jean Nicot, who in 1650 introduced tobacco to France: the drug, of course, known as nicotine.

because successive conquerors always found it useful. As a meeting place, customs house, town hall and even a convent, the temple kept its dignity, but it eventually became a private house of ill-repute and even a stable for thoroughbred horses. In 1576 the Duchess of Uzès tried to buy the Maison Carrée for a family tomb, which roused such hostility that she was fortunate not to have premature need of it. A century later, Jean Baptiste Colbert, controller-general of finance under Louis XIV, commissioned a study on the possibility of having the temple dismantled stone by stone and reassembled at Versailles; but no architect was confident he could put it up again intact.

Inside the temple is an antiquities museum, established in 1821, displaying discoveries from the same period, including a marble statue and a bronze head of Apollo. The statue of Venus was reassembled in 1873 from more than 100 fragments. The original mosaic centrepiece of the floor of the cella is exceptionally well preserved.

West of the Maison Carrée, the quai de la Fontaine alongside a canal leads to the Fontaine Gardens, the creation 1740–1750 of Engineer Mareschal. This was almost certainly an up-market quarter of Roman Nîmes, with a theatre, baths and temple built around the spring. The 2nd-century rectangular Temple of Diana, largely destroyed during the Wars of Religion, was used as a church in the Middle Ages and now provides a setting for summer music festivals.

The footpaths climb 114m to the Tour Magna, a great octagonal tower built by the Romans c15BC on the foundations of an earlier Gallic foundation. Now 30m high, it was originally at least 36m, but the top storey has crumbled away. The exact purpose of the tower is uncertain — it may have been a watchtower, a tomb, or a memorial celebrating some Roman triumph. As Nîmes grew in importance, it was incorporated into the defences as one of the 19 towers in the city's circular wall. Energetic visitors who conquer the 140 steps to the viewing platform, which was restored in 1843, are rewarded by superb views of the city, the Garrigues to the north, and to the south–west occasionally even the

The Maison Carrée, Nîmes: the best-preserved temple of antiquity

Pyrenees on an exceptionally clear day. An uninterrupted view of the Tour Magne itself is frustratingly difficult for would-be photographers to find: try rue Mallarmé to the east. This has the advantage of also being a slightly roundabout route to the Castellum, off rue de la Lampèze, the remains of the Roman water tower. Discovered in 1884, the original collecting basin, 6m in diameter, distributed the water carried over the Pont du Gard (see page 38) by way of ten canal ducts.

The old quarter has been largely closed to traffic. Full of agreeable if expensive boutiques, the pedestrian streets contain a number of exceptional houses, beautifully restored. No 1 rue de la Madeleine has 12th-century origins and an ornate Romanesque façade. No 8 and No 14 rue de l'Aspic have superb staircases, the former Renaissance, the latter 17th-century with a double spiral; No 3 rue de Bernis has a 15th-century façade with mullioned windows and a striking interior courtyard (whose antique style well, however, dates from the 18th century); No 12 rue des Marchands, with its vaulted arches and balustrades, has been turned into an antique arcade.

The Museum of Old Nîmes, between the amphitheatre and the cathedral, was built in the 17th century as a bishop's palace. Some of its 17th-century furniture, notably six prodigious cupboards, belonged to the Church but were saved from plunder because of their size and weight. The museum also contains some beautifully embroidered 18th-century shawls and waistcoats and a collection of regional history. It leads directly into the Musée Taurin, two rooms devoted to bull-fighting, one Spanish, one Provençal style.

The Musée Archaeologique in the rue Admiral Courbet, which borders on Old Nîmes to the east, has an exhibition showing life in the city from the early Iron Age to the departure of the Romans, including toys, toiletries and cooking utensils; as well as a valuable collection of coins. Among some tombs, is that of gladiator Lucius Pompeius, who fought in the Arena in the 1st century AD armed with net and trident. He killed nine successive opponents, only to die in his turn, aged just 25.

At the northern end of the street is the Arles' Gate, known also as Augustus Gate because of its origins commemorated by the bronze statue of the emperor now at its centre. Dating back to c15BC, it consisted of two large arches for chariots and other wheeled traffic, and two smaller arches for pedestrians to pass through on the road to Rome.

The Cathedral of Notre-Dame et St.-Castor stands at the centre of the old town. Built on Roman foundations in 1096, it has been remodelled and restored many times, culminating in almost complete reconstruction in the 19th century. The Romanesque frieze on the west front, with scenes from the Book of Genesis, including Adam and Eve, Cain and Abel, is only partly original. The eight scenes on the left of the façade are genuine, but the rest are copies.

Sommières, 30km south–west on D40, was once a quiet, neglected village whose only rescue from obscurity was the house belonging to the writer, Lawrence Durrell, on the bank of the River Vidourie, Sommières now has somewhat unwelcome fame. It was used by the French film producer Claude Berri as part of the setting (together with Cuges-les-Pin, see Aubagne, page 000, for more details) Aubagne, page 100, for more details) *Florette*, chosen as best film in 1988 by the British Academy. Sommières, however, has much more to offer: delightful riverside scenery, the remains of a walled town, an old tower guarding the single surviving Roman arch of a contemporary bridge, and a ruined castle above. **Nages**, 16km south-west on N113, D107, D345 (or take D40, D737) which has a working Roman cistern, is the closest point by car to **Oppidum**. A major archaeological site, 20 minutes on foot, prehistoric Oppidum had a perimeter wall with gateways and at least three towers. There are exceptional views of Mont Ventoux to the north–east and the Camargue to the south–east. The underground spring at **Perrier**, 15km south–west of Nîmes on N112 and D139, is the source of the great industry that produces more than 600 million bottles a year of the naturally sparkling mineral water.

6

Avignon to Arles and the Camargue

Avignon to Arles

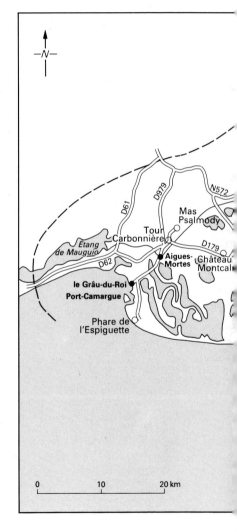

In medieval times, Provence was a dangerous place to be caught on the road after dark. For many travellers, **Barbentane**, 10km south–west of Avignon by D35, was once a place of refuge for those unable to reach the great city in time. Its twin gates, Calendale and Seguier, would be closed at sunset.

The town, on the wooded slopes of the Montagnette, or Little Mountain, a range of tiny hills running parallel to the Rhône. It possessed an imposing castle in its heyday, but only the Tour Anglica survives. This 40m square tower and turret was built in the 14th century and, unusually for this unhygienic period of history, included a latrine on every floor.

Some of the fine houses on the main street date from when Barbentane was a summer residence for members of the Papal court, notably the Maison des Chevaliers, with its loggia gallery running the full length of the façade. The Romanesque church of Notre-Dame-de-Grace, built in the 13th century, was extended in the 15th, including its tower whose bell chamber is decorated with bizarre water spouts.

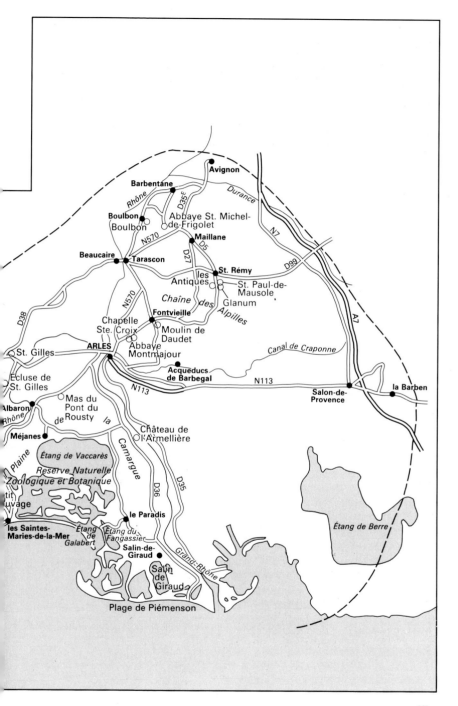

Legends of Tarascon

The Tarasque

When chivalry emerged from the Dark Ages, the economic life of Tarascon was brought to a standstill by the Tarasque, an amphibious monster, half-lion and half-crocodile, that preyed upon anyone trying to use or cross the river. It was particularly partial to the local washerwomen, one of whom was spared and dragged back to the Tarasque's cave, to act for the next seven years as wet-nurse and nanny to its child, called Drac. Sixteen knights were sent to tackle the Tarasque, who defeated them all, devouring eight. The task then befell St. Martha, the sister of Mary Magdalene (see also box, page 102). St. Martha subdued the monster with the aid of holy water and a cross; then, fashioning her girdle into a halter, she led the Tarasque back into the Rhône, where it disappeared for ever.

A huge papier-mâché model of the Tarasque, its tail thrashing, takes part in the annual festival on St. Martha's Day, the last Sunday in June.

St. Martha

St. Martha is said to have been buried at Tarascon, where her remains were rediscovered in 1184, prompting the reconstruction and consecration of the Church of Ste. Martha in 1197. The Church is a mélange of styles, with only the south portal surviving intact from the Romanesque period. The nave is an outstanding example of Provençal Gothic, while its side chapels contain paintings by Nicolas Mignard (1612–1695). As for St. Martha, her relics in the 12th-century crypt now rest inside a 17th-century marble mausoleum.

Tartarin

The town is also the imaginary home of Tartarin, hero of Daudet's famous comic trilogy, *Tartarin de Tarascon*, who fantasised his way through a series of extraordinary adventures. In many ways, he is the archetype of Provençal man as seen by other Frenchmen, warlike in words, but far too concerned with personal well-being and home comforts to participate in hazardous activities. As a result, the Tarasconais became the target of a good deal of cruel French humour, and for a long time refused to acknowledge Tartarin in any way. In 1985 the mood changed, and a house on boulevard Itam was nominated as Tartarin's fictional home. It contains stills of Tartarin in plays and films, and models of the comic hero dressed in some of his fantasy roles. Some visitors leave under the distinct impression that Tartarin was a real person.

However the highlight of Barbentane is its magnificent classical château, overlooking the fields of rich agricultural produce in the Rhône valley. It was built between 1674 and 1678 by Paul-François, Duke of Barbentane, survived the French Revolution undamaged, and remains in the family. The design shows great harmony and simplicity, with two distinct storeys and a broad balustraded terrace leading down to a long rectangular pool. The interior, too, is outstanding, with Louis XV and Louis XVI furniture, and ornate painted ceilings.

South of Barbentane, and reached via D35E, the Abbey of **St.-Michel-de-Frigolet** lies in a fragrant, shady hollow. The aromatic herbs that surround it, including rosemary, lavender and thyme, make it likely that its name is a derivative of *ferigoulo*, thyme in Provençal. Until the end of the 19th century, the monks distilled and sold a herb-based liqueur, not dissimilar to benedictine. The liqueur sold today in the monastery shop is made elsewhere and is probably a lot less potent than the original.

The abbey was where the monks of Montmajour (see Arles, page 56) sent their sick brothers,· victims of marsh fever, to recuperate. They founded its 11th-century Romanesque chapel, Notre-Dame-de-Bon-Remède, Our Lady of Goodly Remedy. The chapel apart, unfortunately little of the medieval abbey survives, as the original monastic order was dissolved during the French Revolution. In 1839 it briefly became a boarding school, whose pupils included the great Provençal poet, Frédéric Mistral (see page 52). The 19th-century reconstruction was the work of the Premonstratensians, the Order of White Canons.

Castle keep at Beaucaire, once the frontier of France

The old road between Avignon and Tarascon winds its way past the village of **Boulbon**, the location of a huge castle built at the end of the 14th century by Louis II of Anjou, governor of Provence. Linked by ruined walls and crumbling towers, it makes extremely ingenious use of the natural rock, and would have been almost impregnable in its day. Many of those who fell in the defence of Boulbon's fortress were no doubt buried in the lovely little Chapelle St.-Marcellin, dating from c1170, on its northern edge. St. Marcellin is the patron saint of wine, and on June 1 each year the men of the village take part in the *fiesole*, the Procession of the Bottles, which winds its way to the chapel for the blessing of the local wine.

49

Frédéric Mistral

Frédéric Mistral (1830–1914) was born on a large farm just outside the village of Maillane, and spent his formative years helping his parents work the land. To Mistral, who later read law at Aix-en-Provence, the contrast between town and country was acute, and he became obsessed at an early age with the belief that Provence's heritage and traditions were in danger of disappearing altogether. In May, 1854, at the age of 24, he persuaded a group of friends, including his former schoolmaster, Joseph Roumanille, and an Avignon publisher called Théodore Aubanel, to found a society whose primary aim was the revival and rationalisation of the old Provençal language. They called themselves the Félibres, after an old Provençal song about comradeship. Following the death of his father in 1855, Mistral sold the farm and moved with his mother to the quaintly named Maison Lezard, in the centre of the village. He could now devote his time almost exclusively to the Félibre cause, and in 1859 produced *Mireio*, an epic poem of Provençal life, which received universal acclaim. In 1876, Mistral married and moved into the house next door, where he soon began work on his magnum opus, a dictionary-cum-encyclopaedia of Provençal words and sayings, *Le Trésor de la Félibre*; it took seven years to complete, and was published in 1886. After 1905, when he was awarded the Nobel Prize for Literature, Mistral was a celebrity: though not, by all accounts, a gracious one, as he discouraged visitors. He would probably have been extremely irritated to find that his house is now a museum, perfectly preserved as the petit bourgeois residence it was at his death in 1914.

When it comes to castles, however, **Tarascon** stands majestic and supreme. Built, like Boulbon, for Louis II of Anjou, between 1399 and 1447 (some sources say 1449) on a rock beside the Rhône, it was a potent message to France that her power ended here. The castle is 100m long and 50m wide in parts, with formidable, battlemented walls of golden stone. Its projecting machicolations and slit-like windows, and a single gateway, protected, in the Middle Ages, by a drawbridge over the moat, lead into a huge outer courtyard, the headquarters of its garrison. But the main castle, a quadrilateral keep, has comfort as well as strength; in its own, inner courtyard, reliefs of King René of Provence and his second wife, Jeanne de Laval, look down benevolently on the scene below. René spent half his reign at Tarascon, and the magnificent seigneurial apartments, complete with en suite royal latrine, emphasise the style and comfort of his surroundings.

In medieval times, when this was the frontier between France and Provence, a second great stronghold at **Beaucaire** counterbalanced Tarascon on the other side of the Rhône. Beaucaire's castle was considerably older, built in the early part of the 13th century by Raymond VI, Count of Toulouse, on the site of an earlier fortification that goes back at least until the 11th century. Just how grand it was, no one knows for certain, as the castle was dismantled stone by stone in the 17th century, on the orders of Cardinal Richelieu, during his campaign to remove the source of Protestant power in the south. Only the shell survives, together with a narrow staircase in the wall that leads to the triangular keep, built into the rock, with its crenellated ramparts at the top.

The romantics among us can imagine this to be the trysting place of *Aucassin et Nicolette*, the medieval lovers whose anonymous tale has survived rather longer than their castle. Aucassin, eldest son of the formidable Count Garin of Beaucaire, falls in love with Nicolette, the Carthaginian slave-girl and booty of the Crusades. Garin is appalled by this social calamity, and locks the lovers in separate parts of the castle. Unusually for a medieval love story, there is a happy ending, as the Count relents and allows Aucassin and Nicolette to marry.

On the tranquil meadow between the castle and the river, Raymond VI also founded an annual fair that was to make Beaucaire from 1217 one of the most famous towns in Europe. For a fortnight every July, the population swelled to around 300,000, with perhaps as many as 700 ships crammed into the tiny river harbour and moored on the bank downstream. On land, whole streets were taken over, indeed renamed, by merchants specialising in particular products. Thus Bijoutiers was Jewellers' Lane; Beaujolais was Wine Street; and Marseillaise the street where the traders of Marseille sold oil, soap, and, nurturing a tradition that was to endure into the 20th century, all kinds of drugs. The fairground on the river bank had everything from dentists to dwarfs, bearded

The antiquities: Triumphal Arch and mausoleum at Glanum

Broken ramparts at les Baux

ladies to performing bears. But its days were already numbered. The coming of the railways revolutionised freight transport, and Beaucaire ceased to be an attractive centre.

A diversion north–east of Tarascon on N570, then south of D5, brings the visitor to **Maillane**, a nondescript agricultural village that would undoubtedly have vanished into obscurity had it not been the birthplace and, for most of his life, the residence of Frédéric Mistral (see box, page 50).

St. Rémy, further south on D5, was the phoenix that arose from the ashes of nearby Glanum (see below). It is best known as the birthplace of Michel de Nostredame, the doctor and astrologer Nostradamus, on December 14th 1503, possibly in the house with mullioned windows on avenue Hoche.

After studying at Montpellier, Nostradamus discovered some remedies for the plague (based mainly on superior hygiene) and fell foul of his colleagues in the medical profession for refusing to divulge his secret. He was later to earn fame and fortune for a series of remarkable predictions of the future in his book *Centuries* (1558). St. Rémy was a wealthy town in the 16th century, constructing arcaded terraces, now occupied by pleasant cafes, and splendid mansions. Among the best are the Hôtel Mistral de Mondragon, built in 1550, and the 15th–16th-century Hôtel de Sade, owned by forerunners of the notorious Marquis. It now contains the Dépôt Archéologique, a collection of antiquities from **Glanum**, best seen after the visit to Glanum itself.

Just north of Glanum, a road to the left leads to the Benedictine monastery of **St. Paul-de-Mausole**, named after the Mausoleum (see below) at Glanum. The earliest surviving parts of the monastery are its 12th-century massive fortified Romanesque bell tower and charming cloister, but the monastery's own records go back to 982, and it probably existed much earlier. The monastic order was dissolved in 1807 during the French Revolution, when it became a lunatic asylum and eventually a psychiatric hospital. Its most famous patient was Vincent van Gogh (see box, page 62), an inmate from May 8, 1889 to May 16, 1890. His cell is no longer open to visitors, but a bronze bust of the great painter stands in the drive.

Where the gates of **Glanum** probably once stood, the crossroads of the Roman way to Spain and Italy, are the 'Antiquities', the Roman arch and mausoleum admired by travellers since the Middle Ages. In the 4th century BC, the Massalian Greeks settled there, building the earliest Greek houses, with columns and peristyles, so far discovered in Provence. After Caesar's humiliation of Marseille in 49BC, Glanum became a health resort, rebuilt in Roman style and enlarged during the reign of Augustus (27BC–AD14).

The earlier of the monuments, a triumphal arch probably celebrating Caesar's victories over Greek and Gaul alike, is believed to have been built around 10BC, which would make it earlier than the Roman arch at Orange. Its corner stones depict the goddesses of victory, and the six-sided panels in

Daudet's mill; he owned it only in his books

The Lords of Les Baux

The warlords of Les Baux are the lords of legend. They claimed direct descent from Balthazar, one of the Wise Men from the East, and carried the star of Bethlehem on their banner. By marrying into the French nobility, what the poet Frédéric Mistral called the 'race of eagles' turned their single fortress into a hundred; 79 still exist, though every one is a ruin.

In the 12th and 13th centuries the castle on its rocky eyrie and the village on the steep slopes below played host to one of the Courts of Love, a highly formalised, highly decorous society. It provided employment for 6,000, including wandering troubadours, composing passionate verses for the ladies of the court. The Court of Love survived any number of scandals and acts of violence. One of the lords of Les Baux seduced his niece, and when she fled, heavily pregnant, to a friendly castle, not only besieged it but caused her chamber to collapse by tunnelling under the castle walls. Another, in prison, summoned his wife to bring a ransom but instead she brought a dagger and used it on him. A third was flayed alive for blasphemy, outside the walls of Avignon.

When the Duke of Guise stayed overnight at Les Baux, the wine flowed freely, and the Duke ordered a cannon to be fired every time he proposed a toast. Eventually he declared his intention of firing the cannon himself. Unfortunately it exploded, and what was left of the Duke of Guise now resides in a tomb at St. Trophime in Arles.

In the 14th century Raymond-Louis de Beaufort, Vicomte de Turenne, used Les Baux as a base for looting the countryside and taking hostages. Raymond would set his table high in the castle and watch any prisoners unable to raise a ransom thrown to their death at sunset.

The power of Les Baux was broken by Cardinal Richelieu, who dismantled its fortifications stone by stone. After a momentary revival in 1922 through the discovery of bauxite, named after the village, its population soon dropped to just 78. Today it is more than 300, with a flourishing tourist industry that attracts more than one million visitors a year.

Although many of the original houses are little more than holes in the ground, the fabric of a few Renaissance houses survive, such as the Hotel des Porcelets, now the Museum of Contemporary Art; and the Hotel des Manvilles, with its tiny Protestant chapel. Higher up, overlooking an exquisite little square, is St. Vincent's Church, which contains the lamb's cart used for the 400-year old *fête des bergers*, a unique celebration of Midnight Mass on Christmas Eve.

From the 13th century donjon, Arles, the Camargue and even Aigues Mortes can be seen on a clear day. But the rest of the castle is simply a heap of rubble. At sunset the last rays of the sun give the gaunt remains a sinister hue, and the slightest wind howls across the battlements, like the cry of the doomed. In this mausoleum of dark deeds, stairways lead to nowhere but the abyss: dizzy, beckoning places where even the sure of foot can sometimes stumble. And if they do, the mocking laughter of the Vicomte de Turenne seems to ring about their ears, as he waits through all eternity for another victim to plunge into the valley below.

The sinister ruins of Les Baux

the vaulting, which are remarkably well preserved, have carvings of Ligurians in chains accompanied by their grief-stricken women.

The so-called Mausoleum is in fact a memorial, built of white stone early in the 1st century AD. It stands 19m high on a richly decorated square pedestal, with a four-way arch, surmounted by a circular colonnade beneath a conical roof. The registers of figures in relief are in a remarkable state of preservation, showing battle and hunting scenes, tritons and sea monsters.

The arch probably commemorates Lucius and Caius Caesar, the sons of Agrippa, groomed by their grandfather, the Emperor Augustus, to inherit the Roman Empire. It must therefore have come as an exceptional blow to Augustus when they died tragically within two years of one another.

A visitor short of time or funds can see the Antiquities quite unrestricted day or night, when they are floodlit. However Glanum has a great deal more to offer. Its methodical and painstaking excavation, which began in 1921, has revealed the site of the sacred spring, a Roman baths, two major temples, a forum, a network of sewers, and several prestigious villas.

D5 towards Arles now enters the **Alpilles**, a frightening land of twisted rock, where, in the Middle Ages, every traveller paid homage to the Lords of Les Baux (see box). Turn right on D17 towards Fontvielle and the **Moulin de Daudet**, a left turn on D33.

Born at Nîmes, Alphonse Daudet (1840–1897) made his name as a writer of pathos about Provençal life, including perhaps his most successful book, a collection of short stories entitled *Letters From My Windmill*. The mill has a charming aspect, located on a rocky outcrop that was once an island in the swamp, overlooking the Rhône valley. Unfortunately from a purist's point of view, Daudet almost certainly never wrote a word of the book in the mill, but simply milked the miller for his stories.

The mill, once ruined, has been restored and is in working order, complete with its sails. On the upper floors is the original mechanism that milled the flour, and an exhibition about the mills of Provence. Below, some of Daudet's personal effects and some first editions of his books are on display.

Farther along D17, the Romanesque **Chapelle Ste. Croix** stands alone on a rock honeycombed with tombs. The building, late 12th- or early 13th-century, is in the form of a Greek cross, with a porch and four apses, topped by a campanile.

Nearby is the partly ruined **Montmajour Abbey**. This former Benedictine Abbey may have been founded as early as the 6th century, on the site of a church dedicated to Saint Trophime, popularly supposed to have used Montmajour as a refuge from the Romans. It was certainly an ideal place of safety, located as it then was on an island in the midst of a dangerous marshland. Throughout the Middle Ages Montmajour's influence was considerable: on Good Friday, as many as 100,000 pilgrims assembled there for the annual *pardon*, to have their sins forgiven.

Near the main door of the great 12th-century Romanesque church of Notre Dame with its single wide nave and transept is the entrance to the crypt, partly hewn out of the rock. It is highly unusual, as its five radiating chapels are not repeated in the church above and the light enters by way of the surrounding ambulatory, unique in Provence. The 12th-century cloister has doubled columns and storied capitals with carvings of bears, camels and other animals.

However it seems that Montmajour's period of peaceful prosperity ended abruptly, as its church was never finished, and in 1360 a battlemented *donjon* was built to deter marauders. The marshes, a second line of defence, were drained by a Dutch engineer, Van Ens, in the 17th century. A brief revival in the 18th century saw the construction by Pierre Mignard of a huge chapterhouse and monks' living, but the monks were turned out during the Revolution. The chapterhouse became a sheep pen and the Abbey an easy prey for scavengers looking for stones to construct other buildings.

The final run into Arles, some 7km via D17, passes through languid, rolling Provençal countryside, where the pace of life has not changed for centuries.

Arles to Aigues-Mortes

Both Greek and Roman came to Arles, once chosen capital of the three Gauls (France, Spain and Britain), a city whose geographical location ensured its pre-eminence, the last bridging point across the lower Rhône. Julius Caesar transferred many of Marseille's possessions and privileges to Arles, whose suburb on the east bank, Trinquetaille, became a great shipyard. Constantine the Great, after his conversion to Christianity, built a palace here.

Earlier, Christians had certainly been thrown to the lions as part of the enter-tainment in the Arena, built in place of an earlier wooden structure CAD46 by Crispus Reburrus, also architect of the Nîmes amphitheatre, which is slightly smaller. A French mathematician has measured the entire seating in the Arles Arena, and reached the untested conclusion that its exact capacity was 23,435. The external dimensions are 136m by 107m. Of the original three storeys, the highest is missing, but the remaining two are supported by 60 arches, decorated by columns, the upper Corinthian, the lower Doric.

As at Nîmes, a canopy shielded the spectators from the sun but at Arles they had the additional facility of scented drinking fountains. Many of the internal rooms are richly decorated with mosaic floors and marble walls,

The Roman amphitheatre at Arles

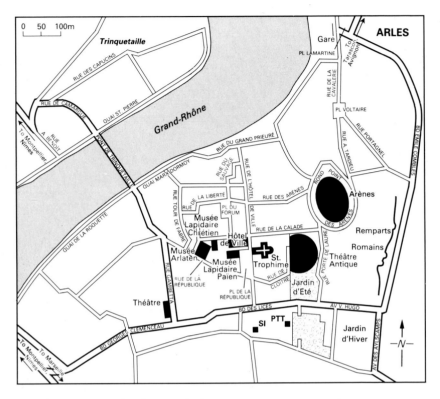

though not entirely for aesthetic reasons: the bodies of dead and mortally wounded gladiators and Christians were brought here during the entertainment, and such rooms were more easily washed down at the end of the day.

After 480, when the legions were withdrawn to the defence of Rome, the amphitheatre became a fortress. By the 12th century a series of stone towers, of which three remain, had been erected on the outer perimeter, which now contained more than 200 houses and a church. In 1825 all the houses were razed to the ground and the Arena excavated.

Upwards and southwest of the amphitheatre, the Roman Theatre was probably built in the 1st century BC

during the reign of Augustus. Now enclosed in an agreeable walled garden, its semi-circular auditorium of 33 rows of seats once had a diameter of 102m. Estimates of its capacity vary between 7,000 and 12,000 spectators. After some restoration, 20 rows of seats remain, together with two huge columns of the proscenium. Plays and other productions are held here regularly during the summer months. In the Middle Ages the theatre became a source of masonry for the city wall and for housing, so much so, that its popular name was 'the quarry'. However much of the damage was done by the early Christians, who mutilated the statues of pagan gods that used to surround the theatre. When a well was sunk in the gardens in 1651, some of

Romanesque octagonal belfry at St. Honorat church, Arles

those statues were discovered, including the famous Venus of Arles. Unfortunately the good citizens made the mistake of presenting the statue to Louis XIV in 1683, and the King ordered the sculptor Giraudon to restore its missing arms. The original, complete with arms, is in the Louvre but copies can be seen at Arles Town Hall and in the Museum of Pagan Art.

To the west, the former Cathedral of the legendary St. Trophime, a supreme example of Romanesque art, was built between 1078 and 1180. The embellishments to the great west portal, reminiscent of a Roman arch, were added between 1180 and 1190. Prominent among its many carved figures are the tall stone saints, with an evocative frieze above them. On its left, the Elect, those chosen to enter the Kingdom of Heaven, proceed fully clothed to have their souls received by an Angel. On its right, the Damned

stand naked in chained despair, pulled remorselessly by a demon towards the fires of Hell. Inside, the barrel-vaulted nave, at over 18m the highest in Provence, also dates from the 12th century. The northern side chapels were added in the 14th, the choir in the 15th and the southern side chapels in the 17th centuries.

The cloister is equally famous for its medieval carvings, revealing Provençal Romanesque at its most creative and beautiful. However only the north and east walks, 12th-century, are in fact Romanesque: the others are 14th-century and have a distinctive gothic style. The most interesting statues, including the saints on the two corner piers, are in the north walk. They date from c1175.

Opposite the former cathedral, the Musée Lapidaire Païen (Museum of Pagan Art), housed in a de-consecrated church, contains an outstanding collection of Greek and Roman statues and tombs. The statue of Augustus (1st century BC) was found in the Roman Theatre, where it is thought to have stood at the rear of the stage. The so-called sarcophagus of Hippolytus and Phaedra, a Greek work of the 2nd or 3rd century, comes from an excavated villa across the Rhone at Trinquetaille.

Nearby, the Musée Lapidaire Chrétien (Museum of Christian Art) concentrates on a display of early Christian sarcophagi, of which the most notable is the 4th-century Tomb of the Trinity. Its occupants, a couple who were evidently extremely rich to have afforded such a memorial, are shown in a medallion underneath a frieze of Old Testament scenes.

From the museum, steps lead down to the Cryptoporticos, a vast underground storage chamber 88m long,

60m wide, built by the Romans under their Forum, though exactly when is uncertain. It contained grain milled (hydraulically — another Roman invention) at Barbegal in the Alpilles, not far from Les Baux. Much of it eventually found its way by sea to Rome, although if the Cryptoporticos leaked as much in Roman times as it does today, the flour could not have been stored for long. During the Second World War, the chamber was used as an air raid shelter.

Slightly farther west, a third outstanding museum, the Museum Arlaten, can be found in a 16th-century Gothic house bought by the poet Frédéric Mistral in 1896. He used the money that accompanied his Nobel Prize of 1905 to complete a unique museum of Provençal life, with more than 30 rooms, showing the artefacts, artistry and everyday existence of a region that was his pride and passion. Many of the traditional costumes and furniture are quite exceptional.

The centre of Arles is best explored on foot, as its maze of narrow streets, full of tourists in summer, have little parking space. However you will need a car to reach the Alyscamps, which is some distance from the centre, in the south-eastern suburbs. The source of almost all the sarcophagi displayed in the Arles museums, a pagan necropolis alongside the Via Aurelia, the Alyscamps was avoided by the superstitious Romans after dark, making it an ideal refuge and meeting place for some of the early Christians. St. Trophime is said to have used it to gather the faithful on his arrival in Arles CAD46. Christ is popularly believed to have joined the congregation for prayer and left the imprint of his knee on a rock.

St. Trophime was allegedly buried at Alyscamps, where miracles reputedly occurred and which took on the mantle of a supremely religious place. From the end of the 4th century, princes and prelates believed Alyscamps to be 'Les Champs Elysées', the Elysian Fields, and asked to be buried here. Soon a vast industry sprang up by which coffins were floated down the Rhône, each accompanied by their burial fee, the *mortellage*, which — some would say by a far greater miracle — survived the journey unscathed. The boatmen of Arles would collect the fees, fish out the coffins, and see them on their way to Alyscamps. By the 16th century, so many tombs existed that the town council of Arles used to curry favour by presenting choice sarcophagi to kings and princes. Unfortunately, they rather overdid a gift intended to be sent upstream in 1570 for the young King Charles IX of France, as the overloaded boat sank to the bottom of the Rhône.

A plaque in the Alyscamps records the spot where Vincent van Gogh painted the burial grounds during his eventful stay in Arles between 1888 and 1890 (see box, page 62).

West of Arles, and second only to the former Cathedral of St. Trophime as a brilliant example of Provençal architecture, stands the **Abbey of St. Gilles**. In the 8th century St. Giles is said to have abandoned all his worldly possessions and set out from Greece on a raft, which carried him to the shores of Provence. Here the hermit-monk made his home in a cave and befriended a doe, which was wounded by Wamba, King of the Visigoths. Wamba would have finished off the deer had not St. Giles plucked his arrow out of the air in mid-flight. This

Cloister of St. Trophime, near Arles

feat so impressed the king that he helped the Saint to found an abbey on the site. St. Giles travelled to Rome to secure recognition for his new order and was presented by the Pope with two huge doors for his ·new abbey. They were too heavy to carry so St. Giles launched them on the Tiber, from where they floated out to sea and were carried to Provence and up river to St. Gilles just in time for the Saint's return.

Much of this story is doubtless apocryphal but St. Giles probably did exist. His tomb, in the 11th-century triple-vaulted crypt, was discovered in 1865, and the age of the remains inside reinforces its authenticity. Most of the original abbey was replaced by a much larger structure in the 12th century, and in particular by the magnificent west front, constructed and carved between 1180 and 1240. Its triple portals, framed by pillars supported on lions, show scenes from the life of Christ. The central doorway is late 12th-century, the work of craftsmen from Toulouse. The outside portals were carved in the early 13th century by sculptors from the Ile de France.

Badly damaged during the Wars of Religion, the eastern part of the Abbey remains in ruins, apart from a solitary bell-tower. It contains a remarkable spiral staircase, known as Le Vis, the Screw, which has the effect of a curved funnel, as its steps are roofed over with stone. This was by any standards a prodigiously ingenious construction, frequently visited through the centuries by stonemasons and their pupils.

Before the creation of Aigues-Mortes (see page 63), St. Gilles was

Vincent van Gogh

Van Gogh (1853–1890), the son of a Dutch pastor, had been a lay preacher himself and later an art dealer before he turned his hand to painting. He was essentially the first artist not a native of Provence to establish himself there deliberately in order to take advantage of the vivid colours resulting from its exceptionally clear atmosphere. However Van Gogh spent much of his stay at Arles in 1888–89 recording the unappealing industrial aspects of the city. The bridge he made famous by his 'Pont de Langlois' was in fact part of a new irrigation scheme, entirely utilitarian and pulled down without a moment's thought in 1926. A copy has been erected at Port-de-Bouc, near Martigues, 40km west of Marseille.

Van Gogh's base was place Lamartine, a down-at-heel area close to the railway station, where he set up his studio in a bistro called La Civette Arlesienne. It was decorated a lurid shade of yellow, painted by Van Gogh as 'The Yellow House'. For most of his stay Van Gogh slept across the square at the Café de l'Alcazar, later the Bar-Restaurant Alcazar. It underwent such a facelift that only the quaint old wall clock survived from the scene painted by Van Gogh in his famous 'Café de Nuit'. His 'Café du Soir' was on the eastern side of the Place du Forum, not far from the Arena. It later became a furniture shop, before being taken over by the Vaccarès Restaurant.

Van Gogh had ambitions of setting up a small colony of artists in Arles, and did persuade his fellow painter Paul Gauguin to join him. Gauguin, however, thought Arles unattractive in the extreme, a view which led the mentally unstable Van Gogh to threaten him with an open razor. The alarmed Gauguin spent the night at the Hotel Camel while Van Gogh proceeded to use the very same razor to cut off his own ear. Gauguin caught the morning train to Paris; Van Gogh committed himself to the lunatic asylum at St. Rémy, where he produced almost 150 pictures during his year-long stay. No sooner had Van Gogh been released as completely cured, in May 1890, than he committed suicide. His last letter to his brother Théo, written just a few months before, concluded: 'My misery will never end.'

the only suitable embarkation point west of Marseille for pilgrims and crusaders bound for the Holy Land. Its trade included spices and perfumes from the Middle East. By the 13th century, the population of St. Gilles was 30,000; by 1925, it was 4,758.

The route from St.-Gilles passes the **Écluse de St.-Gilles**, a lock on the canal linking the Petit Rhône to the Rhône–Sète Canal; and the ruined 18th-century **Château de Montcalm**, whose Marquis was killed by the British in the defence of Quebec in 1759. The parallel old road is soon barred by the **Tour Carbonnière**, a much more formidable defence in the days before the marshes were drained on either side of the causeway. Erected in the 14th century, it was the barbican gate of Aigues-Mortes, complete with its own portcullis and battlements.

The view from the platform, after a climb of 66 steps, is interesting but not recommended, as it will spoil the effect of what is yet to come. After miles of endlessly flat, reclaimed and not yet reclaimed marshes, full of strange, will-o'-the-wisp reflections, tricks of the light, medieval France is reincarnated before our very eyes. A walled city rises on the flat horizon like some desert mirage, **Aigues-Mortes** or 'dead waters', which owed its existence to a benevolent Benedictine Abbey and the religious fervour of Louis IX of France, St. Louis.

Psalmody Abbey was one of at least three vanished so-called 'salt' abbeys (Psalmody is now a splendid farmhouse) whose wealth derived from harvesting the brine crystallized by the sun and the wind on the salt-flats. In 1240 the Abbey was happy to sell Louis the tiny fishing village of Aigues-Mortes and a strip of land that gave him access to the sea.

Louis seems to have been possessed with genuine religious fervour. Although the enthusiasm for the Crusades had faded, he was determined to liberate Jerusalem and organised the Seventh Crusade almost single-handed. However France was far from unified, the Mediterranean ports, such as Marseille, were in the hands of powerful and untrustworthy neighbours, and the King possessed no southern seaboard.

So Louis created a new port, building for its protection the Tower of Constance, which originally had its own moat. A channel was dug to the open sea, nowadays 8km distant. By 1248 it was deep enough to accommodate a fleet of 38 ships, carrying 30,000 men, which set sail for the Holy Land.

Despite his efforts, the Crusade proved a complete fiasco. Louis disembarked in Egypt, where he was taken prisoner. France had to find a huge ransom to secure his release. Undeterred, Louis tried again in 1270: the crusaders set sail for Tunis, where disease decimated the Christian army, and Louis died.

It was left to his son, Philip the Bold, to develop Aigues-Mortes. He dug a second ship channel to the sea, as the first was already silting up, and built a wall around the city. His Italian architect Simone Boccanegra designed the fortifications, rare if not unique in their homogenous construction, completed by 1300. A deep moat surrounded the north wall, and the sea and the lagoon ran alongside the remainder. Even if an army did penetrate the causeway, it was guarded by the strongest gate, the Porte de la Gardette, which had twin towers, huge iron doors, and a drawbridge barred at each end by a portcullis. In contrast, the five small gates in the south wall showed how little Aigues-Mortes feared attack from the sea. The gates here include the Porte de l'Organeau, 'organeau' being the huge iron ring set in the castle wall to which each of the large ships was successively moored. The town contained as many as 30,000 inhabitants, but by the late 14th century the sea had begun to recede and the channels had silted up to a point where they were no longer navigable. France acquired fresh access to the sea through Marseille, and Aigues-Mortes went into almost terminal decline.

The tour of the ramparts usually begins in the north-west corner, at the Port de la Gardette, and passes such intriguing posterns as the Porte des Remblais, the Ballast Loaders' Wicket,

Aigues-Mortes, medieval time capsule

and the Porte des Cordeliers, the Shoe-makers' Wicket. Of the 15 towers, the five largest are called Sel (Salt), Ville-neuve, Mèche (Wick), Poudrière (Powder Magazine) and des Bourguig-nons (the Burgundians'). The Wick was in fact a torch kept constantly alight to ignite the cannons trained on the outer harbour. It was kept safely out of reach of the ammunition stored in the Poudri-ère. The Burgundian Tower takes its name from the gory incident of 1421 during the One Hundred Years' War. The Burgundians took the town through treachery but the royal troops surprised them in their turn and slaugh-tered them to a man. The number of corpses was so great that they had to be temporarily stored in the south-west tower, and covered in mounds of salt to prevent putrefaction.

From Aigues-Mortes, continue south on D979 and D62*b* to **Port-Camargue**, a modern resort started in 1969. Deserted in winter, in summer it offers moorings for more than 3,000 pleasure craft, and bungalow accom-modation. However it lacks the style and imagination of Port Grimaud (see page 123). Beyond Port-Camargue, the tarmac road leads to the **Espiguette Lighthouse**, standing on the edge of wind-swept sand-dunes commanding the Languedoc coast.

On the return trip to Arles, detour to **Le-Grau-du-Roi**, at the mouth of the Grand-Roubine, the modern canal linking Aigues-Mortes to the sea. Once a small, inconsequential fishing port, it has become a popular and picturesque resort.

The Camargue

Arles is also the gateway to the Camargue, a unique region of infertile grassland, melancholy marshes and languid lagoons. Strictly defined as the triangle between the two arms of the Rhône, the Grand Rhône to the east and the Petit Rhône to the west, bounded by the sea, it has come to mean the entire plain between the Étang de Mauguio in the west and the Étang de Berre in the east. For those with the choice, it is best visited in the spring or early summer before the atmosphere is ruined by the sheer weight of tourists, and before the mosquitoes arrive for the blood-letting in autumn.

The Camargue is first mentioned in the days of the early Greek and Roman settlers, when it was entirely different in appearance. The ground was fertile and heavily wooded. The Greeks are believed to have built a temple to Artemis of Ephesus here, but archaeologists looking for its site have discovered only fragments of Greek and Gallo–Roman pottery. The Romans found the area attractive enough for the construction of luxurious villas. The retired soldiers of the Sixth Legion, based on Arles, used the grasslands of the delta for breeding livestock. The 'salt' abbeys of Psalmody (see page 63), Sylvereal and Ulmet were founded in clearings in the woods, whose trees were used for building watchtowers in the marshes and ships on the Rhone. But in the later Middle Ages the supply of wood began to dry up and a series of climatic changes made the region increasingly uneconomic and inhospitable.

What saved the Camargue from total desolation was its fighting bulls and wild horses. The bulls may well have been imported from Greece; the horses probably derived from a breed imported by the Saracens during their incursions into southern Europe, although some weary knights returning from the Crusades had to sell captured Moorish steeds at Aigues-Mortes in order to raise the wherewithal for the rest of their journey. Rounding up these animals was difficult and dangerous, for the marshes were full of treacherous quicksands and bogs into which horse and rider could be swallowed up in seconds. In the 16th century, however, advances in agrarian techniques made it possible to reclaim part of the marshes and to grow rice in the remainder, not at that stage for human consumption but to desalinate the soil and provide feed for the animals.

The men who eked out a precarious and lonely existence in the Camargue were known, then as now, as the *gardiens*. When the weather was too fierce to allow herding bulls on horseback, they would retire to their *cabanes*, white-washed cottages with a cross mounted on the roof, and whose other dominant feature is a huge hearth in the kitchen-cum-living room.

However the ecological changes in the Camargue, particularly in the early 19th century when the Rhône was divided into two branches, aggravating the changes in the context of the soil, made it improbable that the *gardiens* would have survived without outside help. It came from a most unlikely source, an Italian nobleman, the Marquis Folco Baroncelli-Javon.

In 1889 the Marquis inherited property in Florence from the Italian

The Black Bulls of the Camargue

The black bulls roam freely after branding, which takes place at *ferrades*, spectacular affairs where the *gardiens* use their horses to separate the one-year-old steers from the rest and wrestle them on their sides ready for the hot iron. As the bulls become older and more dangerous, they are controlled by *ficherouns*, long, trident-like sticks.

Most bulls are bred to appear at local bullfights, which unlike the *corridas* in the formal rings in the amphitheatres of Arles and Nîmes, are not fought in the gory Spanish manner, ending in the death of the bull. The Provençal *courses à la cocarde* take place in more improvised village rings and the bull survives, though not to fight another day, as the experience it acquires makes it all the more dangerous. After an escorted run through the streets, called the *abrivado*, each bull goes into the ring with a rosette or cockade (hence *à la cocarde*) attached to its forehead by a string around its horns. The bullfighters, dressed in white throughout, have to attempt to retrieve the rosette and the first to do so is the winner. They are known as *razeteurs*, after the *razète* or tight semi-circle they adopt to approach the target, similar to the technique used in a Spanish bullfight by the *banderillo* to plant his sticks or *banderillas* that weaken the bull. In Provence, the bull remains strong and deadly to the last, and more often than not the *razeteur* has to leap the barrier (the *coup de barrière*) to escape a charge. The bull has been known to follow him across the fence into the rows of spectators, so a seat close to the ring is not necessarily to be recommended.

branch of the family, and decided to sell up and become a *gardien* in the Camargue. In actual fact he bought a farmhouse, and left the more disagreeable aspects of Camargue life to the genuine *gardiens*. However he did a great deal to formalise the biennial pilgrimages of the *gardiens* to Les Saintes-Maries-de-la-Mer, and turned them into cult figures not unlike North American cowboys.

The analogy was completed to perfection when Buffalo Bill Cody brought his Wild West Show to Provence in 1889. Pictures were taken of genuine cowboys riding herd on the Camargue bulls, and of the Marquis' farmhouse surrounded by teepees. The tour proved a sensational success, and it ensured that the Camargue, as the next best thing to the Wild West,

was firmly on the map.

The French cowboys still ride in the Camargue, but largely for the benefit of tourists. Breeding the bulls is no longer in itself an economic proposition, and most of the ranches have become hotels and riding centres. Their stocky white horses are born brown and turn creamy white only in their fourth year. Some of them stray and become genuinely wild, feeding off the land.

At least twice a year, usually on 24th/25th May, and on the weekend closest to 22nd October, the *gardiens* make a pilgrimage to the principal centre of the Camargue, **Les Saintes-Maries-de-la-Mer**, a holiday resort almost due south of Arles. In May they are joined in the Pélérinage des Gitanes, the Gipsy Feast, by the gipsies of Europe.

The come to honour the shrine of their patroness, Sarah, said to be the black Ethiopian servant of Mary Salome, the mother of the Apostles James and John, and Mary Jacobe, sister of the Virgin. Believed to have come to Provence on the Boat of the Bethany (see box, page 102), the two Marys and Sarah are said to have built an oratory at Les Saintes-Maries-de-la-Mer and to be buried there.

In the 9th century this oratory was replaced by a fortified church, with loopholes instead of windows, a reflection of the age when the villagers went in fear of the Saracens. In 869 they incorporated the church into the village walls by adding a castellated promenade around its roof.

In the late 11th or early 12th century the church, though still fortified, was replaced by the present Romanesque building, with its austere, dingy nave; its original name was Notre Dame de la Mère. In the second half of the 12th century Queen Jeanne of Provence had a watchtower constructed on the roof over the apse, which has since become the 'Chapelle des Miracles'. It contains what are said to be the relics of the two Marys, discovered when various graves in the church were exhumed in 1448 on the orders of Good King René (see page 7). They also found what are believed to be the remains of Sarah, but as a servant she could not really be buried with her mistresses. Instead, René constructed a crypt to house her reliquary. It is here each May that the gipsies hold a night vigil in her honour, and pay homage to her statue. The following day the pink and blue statues of the two saints are lowered from their chapel to the church altar, and from there borne on the shoulders of the gipsies and taken by boat into the sea. A little band of musicians strike up on their *galoubets*, the triple-holed flutes of Provence; the *gardiens* ride their white horses up to their necks in the waves; and as the Bishop gives the Benediction of The Sea, the crowd on the shore stands in silence. At that moment, it would take a brave man to dismiss the story of the Boat of the Bethany, that the Gospels never told.

About 3km miles west of the town, close to the simple grave of the Marquis de Baroncelli-Javon (see page 65, above). A boat goes regularly in season from the landing-stage on the Petit Rhone as far as the **Petit Sauvage Ferry**. It is a delightful trip, alongside grazing pastures with snorting bulls and frisky horses, and feeding and breeding grounds for heron, duck, and if you are lucky, beautiful flamingos.

However the only European breeding-ground of the flamingo lies to the south-east, a nature reserve of 15,000 hectares, set up in 1928, by François Huet (1905–1972), who lived to see its protected status enforced still more strictly in 1970. Only accredited ornithologists and students are permitted to enter the reserve, which extends around the Étang de Vaccarès and is invaded each spring by migrant birds from many parts of the world.

At **Méjanes**, an electric railway runs along the NW corner of the Lake, the brainchild of the *pastis* millionaire, Paul Ricard. The centre has a large herd of bulls, its own bullring, pony-trekking and a host of other entertainments for children and adults alike.

The road skirting the lake divides at Le Paridis. The seaward loop extends to Pertuis de la Comtesse, just short of the Gacholle Lighthouse, where a telescope in a hide can be used in summer

Wild white horses in the Camargue

to view the pink flamingos. Other birds can be seen from the causeway between the Fangassier and Galabert *étangs*, before the road loops towards Salin-de-Giraud. Just south of the salt pans, where salt is produced by the gradual evaporation of salt water, lie huge white hills of salt.

Although the direct route to Arles is back along D36 by the banks of the Grand Rhône, the road continues south-eastwards to the **Plage de Piemenson**, where the Camargue ends at the Gulf of Lyon. The sand, backed by dunes, is magnificent, but because of fierce currents the sea is extremely dangerous for bathing. On the return journey, pass by way of the **Château de l'Armellière**, 16km south of Arles, a square, towered castle built in 1607. The best museum of the area is located

in the **Mas du Pont de Rousty**, on D570 between Arles and Albaron.

To the south–east of Arles, a grey white desert known as the **Crau** defies the efforts of man or beast to make its home there. At one time it was much larger, a formidable barrier that few travellers would cross. However in 1554 the Craponne Canal was completed, returning the waters of the Durance to their original delta on the Berre Lagoon, allowing the north of the region to be irrigated and reclaimed. The whimsical nature of the Durance is thought to account for the principal characteristic of the Crau, huge rocks and stones, at some points reaching a depth of 15 m, left in an arid delta when the river changed course to become a tributary of the Rhône.

The Crau, and for that matter the

Camargue, are at their worst when the mistral is blowing from the north down the Rhône valley to the Mediterranean shore. It is supposed to be a winter phenomenon but rarely keeps to its calendar. Groves of olive trees hunched like old men testify to its strength, which in summer can fuel fierce and devastating forest fires. In 1775 the mistral blew without interruption for 90 days and nights; almost a century later, it demolished the bridge between Beauclaire and Tarascon. Soon after the single track railway line was built linking Arles to **Port-St-Louis-du-Rhône**, a small port on the east bank dating from 1871, a train completed the 41km journey without an engine — blown by the mistral. What the would-be engine driver, left trainless at Arles, wrote in his report is not recorded.

7
The Lubéron Mountains

If Provence still keeps a secret, it keeps it here: in the Alpes des Lumières, so called because the sun is said to shine almost every day of the year. A hyperbole, perhaps, but the clouds do roll quickly away from the Lubéron Mountains, leaving a marvellously crisp and pure air, and giving the most slothful traveller an appetite for the spectacular scenery. The Grand Lubéron, the wild, exciting eastern range, culminates in the Mourre Nègre, 1,125m above sea

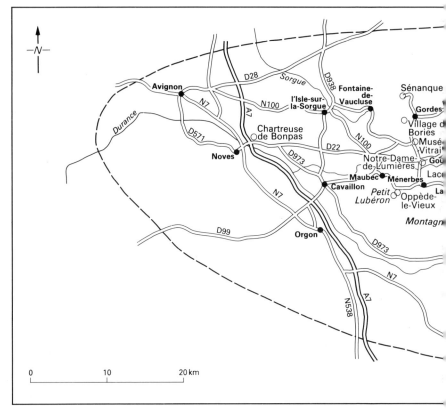

level; the area, now a National Park preserving its superb flora and fauna, can best be explored on foot. The Petit Lubéron, to the east, is largely a fertile plateau where the vineyards jostle one another and the lavender adds a sensational dash of colour. The region is rich in atmosphere, yet for the most part still far enough from the madding crowd.

South–east of Avignon, 10km via N7, D973, lies **Chartreuse de Bonpas**. Travellers attempting to cross the Durance by the ford at this point were warned that it was 'malus passus': not only did the current flow fiercely, but those who struggled to the far bank were liable to be set upon by outlaws.

But with the building of a bridge in 1166, 'malus passus' became 'Bonpas'. The bridge was guarded by the Templars, who in the 13th century built a Romanesque chapel. Its crypt has been carved out of the rock. The Carthusians took over the site in 1320, and erected a chapterhouse in the 17th century; but the monks were turned out during the French Revolution. The terraced gardens offer fine views of the Alpilles and across the river Durance to **Noves**, reached by N7, D28. Supposedly the home town of the beautiful Laura of Petrarch's sonnets (see box, page 86), its 12th-century Romanesque church of St. Baudile has a staircase by its nave that

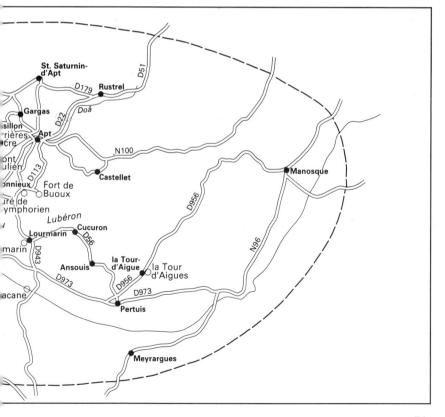

Oppède-le-Vieux, the forgotten village

allowed soldiers to climb directly on to the southern ramparts of the city, a reminder of the constant threat from marauding bands. Further down N7, the ruined castle of Orgon watches over this quiet market town that had its little moment in history at the end of April 1814. On his way to Elba and exile, Napoléon was pulled out of his coach by the citizens of Orgon and made to watch as they burned his effigy on a huge bonfire. Perhaps fortunately for Orgon, when Napoléon returned to Paris less than a year later, he took a different route.

Cavaillon, on the right bank of the Durance, at the foot of the Petit Lubéron, is the centre of the French vegetable industry. From its 'Marché d'Interêt National', the MIN, thousands of tons of produce are transported all over France. The valley is a natural market garden, with such specialities as early asparagus and sweet, pink-skinned melons. Cavaillon's public market operates on Mondays, the big day, and Fridays (try also the *Marché Paysanne* at Castellet, at the other end of the Lubéron range).

In much earlier times, the river was the means of transport, a staging post for the powerful Greek traders from Marseille. Although a Celtic stronghold once stood among the cypress and almond trees of the Colline St. Jacques (a stiff walk up a path from place François-Tourel, but well worth it for the view), Cavaillon was of little military significance to the Romans. This may explain why the small 1st-century Roman Arch of Marius is lavishly decorated but does not record any military 'triumphs', a rare phenomenon. It stands in place du Clos, having survived a move in 1880 from place François-Tourel, stone by stone. The Arch had become embedded in the wall of Notre Dame-et-St. Véran, threatening the stability of the former Romanesque cathedral. St Véran Church, as it is now known, has a 12th-century pentagonal apse and octagonal tower, and an agreeable 14th-century cloister. The side chapels are delightfully decorated with 17th-century paintings and carvings.

The collection of early remedies, not for the squeamish, at the Archaeological Museum, is a reminder that it once housed the town hospital. Most of the huge collection of coins on display were found on the Colline St. Jacques.

Another museum nearby, in the old bakery of a rich 18th-century synagogue, is a reminder of the strong Jewish influence of earlier times. The Avignon Popes tolerated and protected the tiny Jewish communities of Cavaillon, Carpentras, l'Isle-sur-la-Sorgue and Avignon itself ('the Jewish paradise'), a tradition that endured until the French Revolution.

To the south–east, **Oppède-le-Vieux**, so called to distinguish it from the more modern and infinitely mediocre village of les-Poulivets-d'Oppède nearby, is a magical place at the end of nowhere. On the approach road its rows of medieval hillside houses come suddenly into view, balanced precariously on the edge of a rocky outlet in the most obscure part of the Coulon valley. Its colours, its tranquillity, and its fascinating mixture of extravagance and austerity produce a unique atmosphere and a sense of stepping instantaneously into the past. Not, however, without the odd frisson created by the

Gateway at Lacoste: sinister village of the Marquis de Sade

Religious Persecution

A series of religious sects, the Albigensians, the Cathars and the Vaudois, flourished in the south of France, where they challenged the very fabric of the Catholic Church by dispensing with ritual and its role in preparing people for salvation. The Vaudois, called after their founder, a pastor from Lyon named Pierre Valdo, were a tight-knit community living in 24 Lubéron villages. There the sect might have remained but for their own religious zeal, which led to the pillage and burning of local Catholic churches, and an attack on the Abbey of Sénanque. In 1545 the French King, Francis I, spurred on by the Pope, approved a punitive expedition against them. Its leader was Jean Maynier, baron of Oppède, a psychopath whose deeds set him apart even in a cruel and ruthless age. In April he burned five Vaudois villages, taking 800 survivors back to Marseille, where they were sold as galley slaves. At Lacoste, 350 Vaudois women were raped and killed. At Cabrières, 90 villagers were herded into a barn, which was set on fire, burning them alive. At Mérindol, some 200 houses were razed to the ground. Local inhabitants were forbidden to rebuild on pain of death; the parish records were destroyed; and the village was expunged from local maps as though it had been a figment of the imagination.

When Maynier was finally brought to trial for his atrocities in 1551, he was acquitted despite the overwhelming evidence. However seven years later, treated by a mysterious doctor who afterwards disappeared, Maynier died from an agonisingly painful stomach complaint; perhaps the Vaudois had used poison to exact their revenge?

flickering shadows of ancient villainy (see box above).

Oppède-le-Vieux was abandoned in 1910, only to be adopted after the Second World War by a small colony of French artisans and writers. Many of the houses have been restored, and the sharp-eyed visitor taking in the breathtaking view from the terrace of the 11th-century ruined church (firmly bolted), may catch a glimpse of the odd swimming pool nestling among the rooftops below.

The survival of **Ménerbes**, to the north–east, is a tribute to the skills of its stone masons. Hewn out of the north face of the Lubéron, the village was a natural fortress, with a single visible means of access and its own spring water. During the Wars of Religion in the 16th century, Ménerbes was the last stronghold of the Calvinists before they fled into Switzerland. The 1577–78 seige of Ménerbes by the French Catholics lasted 15 months. Unknown to the Catholic troops, its inhabitants were able to come and go as they pleased by way of a secret passage. Much of it has collapsed, but it runs northwards from a vault near the town hall.

The older, upper part of the village remains derelict and largely deserted, a honeycomb of narrow, tapering streets that can trap the unwary motorist. The 13th-century castle, too dangerous to visit, remains an impressive sight with its huge towers built into the confining walls, complete with stone corbels projecting into space and between them a row of machicolations from where boiling oil or rocks were dropped on the besiegers.

In the Romanesque church, rarely open to visitors, the apse has two apparently authentic stained glass windows. However they are in fact painstaking murals, indistinguishable at a distance from the genuine article, quite marvellous artistry. The nearby Jardin de la Citadelle is lovingly tended by an elderly Englishwoman, who with some British companions has rescued the garden from a complete wilderness.

North–west of Ménerbes, the sloping narrow street and pleasant square of Goult-Lumières is overshadowed by the nearby church of **Notre-Dame-des-Lumières**. Lumières became a centre of pilgrimage in 1661 when the ruins of the church were enveloped in a fiery glow of mysterious light, a well-documented event never satisfactorily explained. Soon afterwards a farmer from Goult suffering

The Lord of Lacoste

From a distance, Lacoste looks innocent enough, a verdant hill interrupted by lines of red-roofed houses, nestling beneath a ruined castle. But the single surviving tower, a sinister pinnacle on the skyline, is the key to the village's evil past. For the Lord of Lacoste was once the infamous Marquis de Sade (1740–1814), who used his castle to practise flagellation and sodomy on young girls from the village.

Donatien Alphonse Françoise de Sade, who was of a respected ancient noble family, was orphaned at five and spent his formative years with his reprobate uncle, the Abbot of St.-Léger-d'Ébreuil. Twice accused of sodomy, then a crime punishable by death, de Sade was sent by his family to Lacoste in a vain attempt to escape the authorities. In all he spent 12 years in prison, faithfully recording his perversions in a series of scandalous works. The relaxation of censorship that followed the taking of the Bastille, perhaps combined with de Sade's self-professed though largely imaginary revolutionary zeal, resulted in his release. However in 1801 he was committed to a mental institution at Charenton, where he was to remain until his death, leaving the concept of 'sadism' to posterity.

The Château de Sade, largely destroyed during the French revolution, is approached by a bumpy track above the village. It was acquired in the 60s by a professor from Apt, André Bouer, who spent his holidays in repair and restoration. But two decades have passed, and the scaffolding is still more in evidence than the builders.

The black coach in the de Sade livery may no longer clatter to a halt outside the arched gateway of the single cobbled street, discarding its distraught passenger after a night of terror and humiliation at the hands of the Marquis, but Lacoste still lives in his shadow. Even in the height of summer, the village has an eerie silence, and seems almost abandoned.

from an incurable disease miraculously recovered after claiming to see an angelic child hovering over the church. The church, which had fallen into disrepair, was promptly reconstructed between 1663 and 1669 and stands in a beautiful open woodland setting. The annual pilgrimage takes place on the first Sunday in September.

There is a choice of interesting routes from Ménerbes, either by heading north-east towards Apt, returning to Avignon via Fontaine-de-Vaucluse; or south–east via Bonnieux to explore more of the Lubéron range.

Life in **Bonnieux** has changed little over the last century. Black-garbed old ladies still sit on doorsteps watching the world go by: or gaze with unashamed curiosity through a narrow gap left between lace curtains that frequently rustle but are rarely drawn back. The oldest part of Bonnieux, with fine views through the cedar trees of the Coulon valley, is reached by way of tiny streets, fountains and archways, with some striking front doors, legacies of past affluence and privilege. The 12th-century church is rarely visited, perhaps because its most prized possession, four superb 15th-century paintings from the German School, have been moved to the more modern and unprepossessing church down the hill. Depicting the Martyrdom of Christ, their vivid colours are unmistakable, painted on wooden panels behind the high altar.

Head south from Bonnieux on D36, but then detour north on D943 to **St. Symphorien**, where all that survives of the 11th-century priory, built on limestone rocks in a delightful oak setting, is

Lacoste, home of the Marquis de Sade

Château Lourmarin in the Lubéron

its square Romanesque 12th-century belfry. Turn on to D113 for the natural fortress of **Fort de Buoux**. First used by the Ligurians, then by the Romans, its proper defence works were built in the 13th century. It became a Protestant stronghold during the religious wars until Richelieu ordered its destruction in 1660. Visitors who brave the 1-hour round hike from the road are rewarded by superb views of the Buoux gorge from the ruined ramparts.

Head back to D943, and turn left for **Lourmarin**, once the centre of the Vaudois sect and the first village to be burned by Baron Maynier, in 1541, ahead of his punitive expedition (see Oppède, pages 73–4.) Lourmarin still has a somewhat eccentric 15th-century château that encourages only 'serious' visitors (defined as 'writers, designers and researchers').

In the valley of the Durance, just south of the Lubéron, the Cistercian Abbey of Silvacane is within easy reach of Lourmarin — south on D943, then east on D561. The youngest of the 'three sisters of Provence', the others being Le Thoronet (see page 122) and Sénanque (see page 82), Silvacane stands beside the village of La Roque d'Anthéron. Founded c1147, its name comes from the Latin *silva canorum*, meaning 'forest of reeds', a reference to the marshlands that had to be cleared before the Abbey could be built. The height of its prosperity came in the latter part of the 13th century, when most of its buildings were completed, only to be pillaged and burned in 1357. Aix Cathedral took over the Abbey and built a new refectory in 1420; but the monks disliked their new masters and left. Silvacane became the local parish church and after the Revolution was turned into a farm. The main feature of the Abbey, substantially restored in the mid-19th century, is its high vaulting.

Cucuron, east of Lourmarin on D56, has a ruined 15th-century château, old houses, a Museum of the Lubéron range, and is the starting point for a 20km return hike to the crest of the Grand Lubéron.

Ansouis, a perched village south of Curcuron, at one time existed almost entirely to service the Château de Sabran, unusual in that it has belonged to the same noble family for the last six centuries. When they took over the castle, it was almost entirely medieval and heavily fortified, but as the importance of walls and ramparts diminished, they added an imposing baronial hall.

Eight kilometres east of Ansouis, via Petruis on D56 and D956, **la Tour d'Aigues** offers fine mountain views. The village was once dominated by a splendid Renaissance castle, the pride of Provence. Only the great stone doorway remains intact, as the remainder was deliberately destroyed by fire during the French Revolution. But the frieze of trophies in high relief separating the two stories shows how magnificent an edifice it must have been in its heyday. Indeed, much of the stonework can be seen piecemeal on the older houses of enterprising citizens of la Tour d'Aigues.

Both D3 and D93 are attractive routes from Bonnieux to Apt. To see the best preserved Roman bridge in the whole of France, though, detour on the D149 north of Bonnieux. Just before this road strikes N100, the hump-back **Pont Julien** crosses the River Coulon. Built in the first century AD to carry the *Via Domitia*, one of the principal Roman roads in Provence, it was no mean undertaking, as the Coulon was a much more formidable river than it is

today. The Roman engineers solved the problem of its spring turbulence by boring holes in the arches of the bridge, which is 68m long, 14m high, so that the water could flow freely. The full beauty of the structure can best be appreciated by walking along the north bank of the river for about 100m and looking back at the bridge.

To the north is **Apt**, one of the oldest Provençal towns, distinguished for its contribution to Christianity. The ancient cathedral of St. Anne, started in the 11th century, completed largely in the 14th, but altered again in the 18th, was the first holy place in France to be dedicated to the mother of the Virgin Mary. Indeed, it may have been the earliest in the whole Western world, for archaeological evidence suggests that Christianity was celebrated nearby as

Pont Julien: superb Roman bridge

early as the fourth century. The chapel sacristy displays what is claimed to be the shroud and relics of St. Anne, said to have been buried on the site, whose ancient mystical significance is underlined by the presence of a pagan altar in the lower crypt. The relics are believed to have been discovered in 776, when the original church, built on the foundations of the temple to Augustus, was spring-cleaned in anticipation of a consecration visit from the Emperor, Charlemagne.

At any event, Apt became a popular destination for pilgrims, including Queen Anne of Austria, who came to pray at the altar to be made fertile. A procession celebrates this royal pilgrimage each year on the last Sunday in July. St. Anne's Chapel apart, Apt is of little architectural merit; however it is a useful shopping centre, particularly for local vegetable produce, crystallized fruits, nougat and lavender essence, specialities of the district.

Nearby is the interesting **Colorado de Rustrel**, iron-oxide quarries, 11km north-east on D22, then an unmarked road opposite D30A. Leave the car near the Doa stream, then follow the signs on foot for the best part of an hour to see the giant mushrooms, in fact columns of red ochre topped with huge blobs of clay. Some of the quarries are still working, but the canyon can be viewed safely from the terrace above.

At **St. Saturnin d'Apt**, 8km north of Apt on D943, the 15th-century Porte Ayguier is the only surviving evidence of what was once a walled hamlet, overseen by a medieval castle, now in ruins. It has a Romanesque chapel in a charming setting of cypress trees.

Sunset at Roussillon

D2 and D227 bring you to the famous village of **Roussillon**, so-called after the hue of its houses, whose roofs and walls, a kaleidoscope of ochre-based colours, can be seen for miles. Roussillon lies at the apex of the hills between the Coulon valley and the plateau of the Vaucluse, the centre of a flourishing, though now defunct, quarry industry, whose pit faces in every shade of ochre created an unintentionally artistic masterpiece. The most striking, a jagged array of rose-red cliffs known as the 'Giants' Causeway', is reached by way of the D149 out of Roussillon, a 1hr return walk, left of the cemetery. The best view of the village is, in fact, via N100 and D149; but one of the finest colours, an astonishing red-brown whose intensity seems to increase at sunset, can be seen more easily from the ruined castle keep.

Roussillon's contribution to the colour spectrum, and its clambering network of little streets, have long attracted artists· of all ages. However these days they are not content simply to paint, and the village, especially in summer, has an unending sequence of picture exhibitions designed to open a visitor's purse. Once a quiet, sleepy village, Roussillon has come alive in a fashion not calculated to please the purist. In the peak season, its roads and cafés are jammed with visitors, and seekers of solitude should go elsewhere.

West of Roussillon is **Gordes**, a spectacular Acropolis on a steep rocky hillside. When the village was all but moribund from the 1920s, the French artist André L'hôte put it back on the map. It had a further set-back when the 11th-century Renaissance château, built on the site of an ancient fortress, was wrecked by the Germans in 1944; but the Hungarian artist Victor Vasarély funded the restoration work in return for space to house his museum of didactic art, over 1,000 works with a theme of continuous movement. A more traditional masterpiece of earlier vintage, an ornate Renaissance chimneypiece, can be seen on the first floor of the château. Gordes is now a thriving, if over-priced, craft centre, with artisans' stalls set up outside medieval terraced houses. The superb views over rolling countryside make this an ideal starting point for outings on horseback, a local speciality. Parking is forbidden in the centre of the village: use the car parks at the entrance.

Just 5km north of Gordes stands the great Cistercian Abbey of **Sénanque**, founded by St. Bernard in 1148. Sénanque's remote location (reached via D15 and D177) in a deep, rugged valley, is served by an uncompromising road that was little more than a mule track until the last century. However, this did not prevent its sacking by Protestants from the Vaudois in 1544. Several of the monks were hanged from the walls, an event which led, directly or indirectly, to Maynier's punitive expedition (see page 74) a year later. Disposed of during the French Revolution, it was reacquired by the Cistercian movement in 1854 and lovingly restored. The atmosphere is a unique blend of modern bustle, for this is an active religious centre, with all the trappings of a 12th-century monastery. The medieval kitchens, the monks' dormitory with its cross-cradled Romanesque vaulting and tiny windows, and its tranquil arcaded cloister, have effectively suspended time itself.

Sénanque is one of three famous 'sisters of Provence' founded by the

The Cistercian abbey of Sénanque

Cistercians in the 12th century, with the abbeys of Silvacane (see page 78) and Le Thoronet (see page 122). Sénanque also has a permanent exhibition covering every aspect of the Sahara Desert: incongruous, but interesting.

The **Village of the Bories** is 4km south–west of Gordes, just past the junction of the D15 and the D2, via the D2 and a seemingly interminable unmade track. *Bories* date back to Ligurian times, and are made by stacking rough stones at an angle in ever decreasing circles to create a beehive shape, with the final stone sealing the top. Without mortar and modern tools to shape the stones, today it seems well nigh impossible. Unique to the slopes of the Lubéron and the Vaucluse plateau, most *bories* are to be found in splendid isolation, used by agricultural workers or incorporated into garden walls. Some of them, like this village, were inhabited until the early 19th century, a refuge from religious persecution, conscription, and the plague. It has an interesting museum of traditional country life. Also worth a brief visit is the **Village Noir**, 2km west of Gordes, via the D15 to Cavaillon, and an unclassified road leading to a car park. The so-called Black Village consists entirely of deserted *bories*.

Investigate also **Les Bouillons**, 5km south of Gordes, close to the crossroads of the D148 and D103, a 16th-century mill whose principal claim to fame is a huge olive oil press made from the trunk of a single oak. Next to the mill a modern building accommodates the **Musée du Vitrail** (Museum of Stained Glass) set up by the artist Frederick Duran, part history, part sales outlet, with a small artificial lake garnished with beautiful heather.

There are two sound reasons to

travel south to visit **Fontaine-de-Vaucluse** in the late winter or early spring. First, because the fountain which gives Vaucluse its name is in fact a giant, natural overflow pipe for the river Sorgue which needs heavy rain or melting snow for its spectacular effect. Second, because Vaucluse receives the best part of 1.25 million visitors a year, and most of them come when there is comparatively little to see, turning the marvellous setting into an unromantic tourist trap.

If you must go in the summer, go early. The seductive car park is in fact a long walk from the centre of the village, itself another formidable hike to the cavern where the Sorgue does its stuff in the winter months. But before 1.30pm it is often possible to find a parking space on rue Fontaine, the riverside road leading to the gorge, with the added advantage of by-passing the row of expensive souvenir shops. From here a narrow path — safe enough, though, for children and the elderly — leads to a lagoon-like cavern at the foot of a tall limestone cliff. In summer, the water lies dank and still but in the wet season it pours out of the darkness over the lip of the cavern in a foaming cascade, turning the serenity of the Sorgue into a rushing torrent.

Even in periods of acute drought, the seasonal volume of water — which can reach 150,000 litres a second — never varies, and its temperature does not change by more than one degree from 12.7°C, irrespective of the surrounding air temperature. Experiments using florescent substances placed in potholes in the Lubéron

Gordes, the French acropolis

The Cistercian Abbey of Sénanque; the refectory

mountains and the plateaux of the Vaucluse have shown that the water travels for many miles underground before emerging at Fontaine-de-Vaucluse, although the exact route remains unknown. Efforts to explore the cavern began back in March, 1878, when an Italian diver called Ottonelli, based in Marseille, descended to a depth of 35m to reach a narrow fissure in the cavern similar to the U-bend in a soil pipe. In more modern times, Jacques Cousteau led a 1950 expedition that nearly ended in disaster at 60m when Cousteau and a colleague became disorientated and barely escaped with their lives. It was 17 years before Cousteau was prepared to try again, this time using a robot diver, which reached a depth of 106m, only to find a second sump-like obstruction.

In 1981 another Marseille diver, Claude Touloumdjan, went down to 153m but had to spend seven hours in the icy water on essential decompression. Finally, in 1985, another robot device descended to 309m but still with no sign of reaching the bottom. It seems unlikely that anyone will ever do so.

The river has turned **l'Isle-de-la-Sorgue**, south–west on D25 and D938, into a series of islands, crossing and re-crossing the streets as it divides itself into five branches. Plane trees line the banks of the Sorgue, adding to its charm and tranquillity. Except, that is, in July, when for two nights the river becomes a centre of dazzling colour and inspiration at the Festival of the Sorgue. A procession of floats, which for once can be taken literally, are propelled up and downstream by gondolier look-alikes, to win the applause of the spectators and the votes of the judges. Each float carries its own power supply, so the lights can be switched on and off for maximum effect, enhancing each entry, assembled by schools and families determined to outdo one another with their creative tableaux. A battle of flowers provides the climax of the second evening. A fair and a well patronised outdoor roulette wheel operate alongside the festival for good measure. Arrive early and claim a riverside place for a good view.

L'Isle-sur-la-Sorgue has a beautiful Baroque church whose interior is richly decorated with what appear to be Italian panels, though the artists were in fact Provençal. The old hospital has an elegant fountain in the courtyard, Moustiers pottery jars in the pharmacy, and 18th-century wood-carvings in its chapel. The fine houses dating back to the 16th and 17th centuries are a reminder of the heyday of the silk industry, when the factories were supplied by power from six watermills. All have survived, but just one old water wheel still turns in a public garden.

Petrarch and Laura

The Italian poet, Francesco Petrarch (1304–74) first came to Fontaine-de-Vaucluse in 1337 to muse upon his allegedly unrequired passion for Laura, one of the great love stories of the age. No one can be certain of the identity of Laura, but she is believed to have been Laure of Noves, a small town south-east of Avignon. Petrarch belonged to an affluent family of clerics that had sought refuge in Avignon from the perils of Italian politics. He was 24 when he first caught sight of Laura in the Church of St. Clara, now demolished, on Good Friday, April 6, 1327. Alas, she had been married just two years earlier to Hugues de Sade, ancestor of the infamous Marquis de Sade (see box, page 75). Pretrarch apparently had to be content to worship Laura from afar in a little house, long since disappeared, in the old village of Vaucluse where he lived with 'few servants and many books.'

Petrarch's *canzonei* was startling for its time, Renaissance man defying the conventions of an autocratic church by publicly confessing spiritual love for a married woman. His sonnets fall naturally into two parts. *In vita de Madonna Laura*, written when Laura was alive, and *In morte de Madonna Laura*, after she died of the plague on April 6, 1348, aged about 34.

However Petrarch was no unworldly virgin: he fathered two illegitimate children by another lady in Avignon. As for Laura, she had no fewer than eleven children, despite the fact that Hugues spent a good deal of his life away from Provence. In 1342 some early admirers of Petrarch's poetry made the pilgrimage to Avignon to see the legendary Laura for themselves and found her far too worldly for their taste. Quite what Laura felt about this level of notoriety we shall never know, but it was perhaps just as well for Petrarch that Hugues de Sade was no lover of poetry.

The waters of the fountain at Fontaine-de-Vaucluse

8
Aix-en Provence and Environs

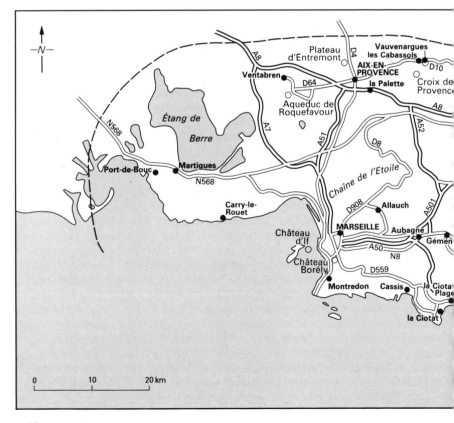

Aix-en-Provence, city of Mirabeau's oratory and Cézanne's canvases, owed its origin to Rome's territorial ambitions. By the end of the 3rd century AD, it was the capital of Gaul. Indeed, given its prestigious past, it is difficult to understand why so little of Roman Aix survives, in view of the durability of the remains at Nîmes and Arles.

When Provence became officially part of France in 1481, Aix remained its capital with its own Governor until 1790, when the city was still in its heyday. Nobles, high churchmen, magistrates and leading burghers all vied with one another in the size of their retinues and the splendour of their

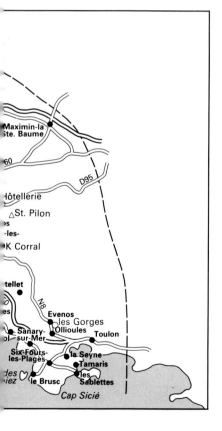

hôtels, mansions or town dwellings. In all, some 70 survive, with some of the finest lining one side (the other has prestigious shops and cafés) of the cours Mirabeau, arguably one of Europe's finest streets. Named after Gabriel Mirabeau (see p. 94), it was constructed between 1649 and 1751 after part of the original Roman wall had been pulled down to clear the way, by well-meaning yet misguided town-planners. It is shaded by four rows of huge plane trees, among the largest and oldest in France, which stretch majestically across the street to form a cool, verdant canopy.

Pâtisserie shops are a particular feature of the cours Mirabeau, selling calissons, an Aix speciality. They are sweets made from almonds, and melon and fruit preserves, originally given away in church on major feast days. Aix leads Europe in almond production.

The street has no fewer than four fountains, including the Fontaine Chaude from which, as its name implies, spurts the warm thermal spring water of Aix; and the Fontaine du Roi René, with a 19th-century statue of the King (see also page 7) holding a bunch of the muscat grape he introduced to Provence. Indeed the city is full of fountains: among the most impressive is the Fontaine de la Rotonde, erected in the epoque of Napoléon III where the cours Mirabeau meets the other main avenues of the city. But the most delightful is the Fontaine de Quatre Dauphins, built in Italian style by Jean-Claude Rambot in 1667. It stands in a peaceful square of the same name, surrounded by more 17th-century *hôtels*, another marvellous microcosm of the great days of Aix.

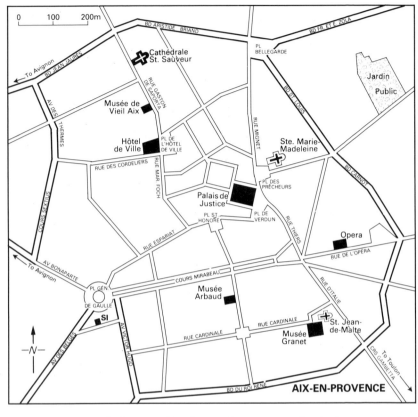

In rue Gaston de Saporta, No 17, the Hôtel d'Estienne de St.-Jean, with a most prestigious grand staircase, accommodates the Museum of Old Aix. Of particular interest is an exhibition based on the Corpus Christi celebrations introduced by King René. At No 19 is the palatial Hôtel de Châteaurenard, where Louis XIV stayed on a visit to Aix in 1660.

In rue Cardinale stands the Gothic Church of St.-Jean-de-Malte, the burial place of the Counts of Provence. Next door, in the old priory, dating from c1675, is the Musée Granet, containing both art and archaeology, notably the collection of decapitated Celto-Ligurian heads discovered at Entremont.

The museum also has an outstanding collection of Provençal faïence. The pictures include works by Jacques Louis David, François Clouet and Dominique Ingres.

One of the two most notable works of art in Aix can be found in the nave of the gothic cathedral of St. Sauveur: the 'Triptych of the Burning Bush'. It was produced by Nicolas Froment, King René's court painter, around 1476. Froment embellished the Biblical text of God appearing to Moses in a burning bush, and placed in its midst the Virgin and Child. The two side panels show René and his queen,

St. Sauveur's Cathedral, Aix-en-Provence

Count Mirabeau

Honoré-Gabriel Victor Riquetti, Count of Mirabeau, was born on March 9, 1749 at the Château de Bignon, in the Île de France. The doctor wrote that he was an ugly child with a twisted foot who 'will certainly have difficulty in speaking'. As a diagnosis of probably the greatest orator France has ever produced, it was somewhat wide of the mark.

What Gabriel lacked in looks, however, he compensated in boldness. After years in disgrace, in December, 1771, he became master of the family château at Mirabeau, where he put down a revolt amongst his retainers with a ruthlessness that ill befitted a future champion of liberty.

Short of money, Mirabeau seduced and married Émilie de Marignane, a plain but rich heiress. When her father refused him funds Mirabeau simply mortgaged his future prospects and ran up debts of £1.5 million. Imprisoned in 1775 in the Château d'If, off Marseille (see page 99), Mirabeau promptly seduced the wife of the governor and was hastily transferred to Fort de Joux at Pontarlier. At a dinner party held by the commandant to show off his famous prisoner, Mirabeau met 20-year-old Sophie de Monnier, married three years earlier to the ageing Marquis de Monnier, and together they eloped to Amsterdam. The Marquis pursued them relentlessly. Mirabeau was extradited to France and condemned to be beheaded for rape by seduction. Though the sentence was revoked, when he returned to his family château, Mirabeau was shunned by society and sued for divorce.

After a period abroad in Berlin, Bath and London, Mirabeau rose to prominence in Paris, making money as a pamphleteer and fierce critic of the increasingly bankrupt and corrupt French government. The king was forced to recall the assembly of nobles, clergy and commoners, the Estates-General. In January, 1789, Mirabeau frustrated a political plot in Provence to deprive the common people of representation. He became the hero of the hour, and was elected to represent Aix, where the people heralded him as 'the father of our country'. In Paris, on June 23, 1789, Mirabeau inspired the commoners, the Third Estate, to refuse to accept the orders of the King. The Revolution that was to take Louis XVI to the guillotine had begun.

However Mirabeau's position was a mass of political contradiction. The aristocracy detested him as a renegade, and the common people distrusted him as an aristocrat, burning down his family château. Mirabeau died of a stroke on April 2, 1791 and was buried with full honours in the Panthéon at Paris. But in 1794, when his schemes to save the monarchy were discovered, his remains were disinterred and thrown into an unmarked ditch in the old cemetery of Clamart.

Cézanne

Paul Cézanne (1839–1906) was born in Aix, at 28 rue de l'Opera, the son of a wealthy milliner money-lender. The family then lived at 14 rue Matheron and later on the cours Mirabeau (see page 91) itself, until Cézanne's father purchased a large 19th-century mansion, south-west of the city, in 1859. In this rural atmosphere of relaxed affluence, Cézanne's passion for art was tolerated but not encouraged. His family regarded his methods as amateur and sent him to art school in Paris, where he acquired technical sophistication, without ruining his highly original style.

With his restrained use of colour and tone, Cézanne certainly achieved his ambition of making Impressionism both credible and durable. However, he was constantly in debt, accepting low prices for his pictures, which if exhibited in Paris would have brought him a fortune. Cézanne was simply not prepared to endure the conversation of the bourgeoisie and felt ill at ease in smart society. He was happy only when he was with a simple crowd of Aix provincials, in the unpretentious Caf' Clem, at No 44 cours Mirabeau. The death of his father in 1886 freed Cézanne of any financial worries. He immediately married his long-suffering mistress, Hortense Fiquet, whom he had met in Paris, and by 1899 they were living in a rented apartment in Aix, at 23 rue Boulegon, where Cézanne died in 1906.

From 1902, Cézanne had travelled each day to a studio in the north of the city at 9 chemin des Lauves, now avenue Paul Cézanne. His studio, facing north on the first floor, has been preserved exactly as he left it: palette, easel, pipe and beret, and the wine bottle he had abandoned, half-empty, the night before. Sadly, though, there is very little of his actual work to be seen in Aix.

Jeanne de Laval. The heavy-jowled René is an unflattering portrait, but when Froment painted him, he was about 65, an old man by medieval standards.

For the other great painting, visit the church of Ste. Marie-Madeleine in place des Prêcheurs. In the north aisle is a wonderful 15th-century triptych of the Annunciation, with the Virgin in dazzling gold brocade. The side panels are copies, as the originals are in Amsterdam and Brussels.

The town hall, in the Place de l'Hôtel de Ville, is bordered by yet another fountain, of 1755 vintage. The Hôtel de Ville itself was designed by Pierre Pavillon in an Italianate style and constructed between 1652 and 1668. On the first floor can be found the library bequeathed to Aix in 1787 by Jean-Baptiste Piquet, Marquis of Méjanes, and first consul of Aix. It contains over 300,000 books and 1,600 manuscripts, including the beautiful Book of Hours, whose wonderful illuminations were certainly created for King René.

Some 15km west of Aix, on D64, the elevated village of **Ventabren**, above the Valley of the Arc, is dominated by the ruins of Queen Jeanne's castle — not Queen Jeanne, the wife of King René, but the far less salubrious

Queen Jeanne of Naples (see Avignon, page 19). There are superb views of the Étang de Berre from the summit. The road from Aix passed the **Aqueduc de Roquefavour**, 85m high, 365m long, built between 1842 and 1847 to carry the waters of the Durance Canal to Marseille.

North of Aix, 3km via D14, lies the plateau of **Entremont**, the Salian stronghold destroyed by the Romans in 123BC (see page 3). Archaeological excavations, which are continuing, have so far uncovered a gateway and parts of houses and of the ramparts.

Mont Ste.-Victoire, 8km north–east of Aix on D10, consists of a white, limestone plateau, whose barren shape became immortalised in the paintings of Cézanne. To reach the top, a demanding 2-hour ascent on foot, park beyond a series of artifical lakes at the farm of Les Cabassols. Take the mule-track to the 17th-century **Priory Notre-Dame de la Victoire** and then on to the monument, the **Croix de Provence** (945m). On a clear day, there are superb views over the Camargue and towards the Alps.

Marseille and Environs

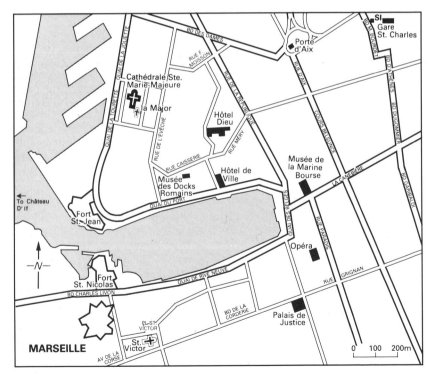

The third, and oldest city of France, home of lost and controversial causes, at once exciting and dangerous, Marseille has a special magic of its own. Founded by the Greeks as Massalia c600BC, the city made the mistake of backing Pompey against Julius Caesar during the Roman civil war: Caesar turned Massalia into a political eunuch, removing its walls, its weapons and its warships. Having rid itself of the Saracens, who sacked the port in 838, Marseille did not profit from the Crusades as much as has been often suggested. Indeed, in an attempt to drum up business, Marseille acquired a whole district of Jerusalem as quarters for the crusaders: one of

Marseille harbour

Fort of St. Jean — Marseille harbour.

the earliest recorded examples of the package tour.

Although, by the 18th century, union with France had stimulated trade, Marseille remained vulnerable to death and disease. In 1720 a virulent plague was carried on a ship from Syria; and more than 50,000 inhabitants died in a matter of months.

During the French Revolution, Marseille was at first against the Revolutionary Convention, but then its own version of the Terror endured long after the fall of Robespierre in Paris, with ever increasing atrocities. Marseille's penchant for backing the wrong horse continued under the Empire when, hard hit by the English naval blockade, the city became

Royalist. No sooner had Louis XVIII been restored than Marseille declared for Napoléon — just in time to see him exiled much more emphatically at St. Helena.

The opening of the Suez Canal in November 1869 enabled Marseille to profit from the faster route to India and the Far East, becoming once again the pre-eminent French port. In the second half of the 19th century its accumulated wealth was used to create many of the buildings that dominate the city, including the Cathedral, Notre-Dame-de-la-Garde, the Stock Exchange and the Gare St.-Charles. It must be said however that the ecclesiastical buildings are no architectural masterpiece and that the station's grand staircase, complete with marble statues, is cursed by many a traveller loaded down with luggage.

The entire Quartier du Vieux Port no longer exists. In 1943 the Germans gave its 40,000 inhabitants 24 hours to depart, and blew the district to bits. Amid the rubble, the remains of the original Roman docks of Massilia emerged: complete with storage jars for the great grain trade, and the odd anchor fished out of the bay.

Although still the home of the Marseille fishing fleet, and a daily fish market, nowadays the old harbour is less of a commercial centre than a congested anchorage of luxurious yachts. From the nearby quai des Belges, motorboats leave twice every daylight hour in season for the Château d'If, passing two notable forts guarding the harbour entrance, the Fort St. Jean, dominated by the Tour du Roi René, a square tower built by King René between 1448 and 1452, and the 17th-century Fort St. Nicholas, whose star-shaped defences were completed in 1668. Château d'If is the single most popular tourist attraction in Marseille. Its principal claim to fame was as the prison that contained The Man in the Iron Mask (see page 131) and the Count of Monte Cristo. At the risk of reducing the fascination of the visit, it must be said that the former never stayed there, and the latter (the hero of Dumas' novel) never existed.

The return journey to the old port offers a magnificent panorama of the city. The Canebière, the main street of Marseille, runs up from the quai des Belges. Its broad pavements are still lined with cafes, but its heyday is past: the traffic has destroyed the ambience. After 7pm it stands desolate and abandoned. Even the Marseille police force

— reliably reported to be the embodiment of that famous old cliché, the best police force money can buy — to all intents and purposes goes off duty and the alleyways of the African *souk* quarter take on a menacing air.

During the day, apart from the occasional pickpocket, crime is no more prevalent than in any large city. However Marseille has its share of urban decay, including even Le Corbusier's Unité d'Habitation, built between 1947 and 1952 off the boulevard Michelet, east of the Old Town. From a distance, this innovative masterpiece that spawned many hideous tower-blocks seems to hover above the ground on sculpted, load-bearing pillars, a vertical space-ship on the launching pad.

South of Marseille, Château Borély is reached by way of the Corniche President J.F. Kennedy. The Château, in early neo-Classical style, was built between 1767 and 1778 for a prodigiously rich Marseilles merchant, Louis de Borély. Much of its original decor has been preserved, particularly in the private appartments of de Borély on the first floor, including his bedroom and chapel.

Marseille's Archaeological Museum is housed on the ground and first floors, including precious mummies, wonderful amulets and scarabs. In the outhouses of the Château, the Lapidary Museum has recently taken on much greater importance, because of its exhibition of finds from Roquepertuse, an archaeological site west of Aix-en-Provence, near Velaux.

On the Château terrace stands a statue of Marseille's most famous sculptor-architect, Pierre Puget (1620–1694), very much a prophet without honour in his native city. Exactly what

*The grim prison of the Château d'If,
Marseille*

Marseille missed can be seen in the Musée des Beaux-Arts in Boulevard Longchamp, where three rooms are devoted to the sculptor's life and his great scheme, sadly rejected, that would have given the city one of the most magnificent squares in Europe.

To the north–west of Marseille, the wild, pine-clad limestone range of the Chaîne de l'Estaque separates the Berre lagoon from the Mediterranean, with few visitors and many fine views. **Carry-le-Rouet**, 32km west of Marseille (via N568 and D5), is a sophisticated small resort with smart villas, mainly frequented by prosperous Marseillais at weekends and in school holidays.

Inland, some 8k farther on D5, **Martigues** stands at the inner entrance to the Canal de Caronte. Martigues' charming old quarter was the subject of 19th-century paintings by Camille Corot and Felix Ziem, whose stay is commemorated by a small museum. The centre, trisected by extensions of the main canal, has a 17th-century church on each section, reflecting rivalries of earlier times. The finest specimen, L'Église de Sainte-Madeleine, stands on the Ile de Brescon, close to the picturesque Pont St. Sebastien.

Port-de-Bouc, at the entrance to the Canal de Caronte, is guarded by a 17th-century fort. Once a quiet port noted for its fish-drying factory and boatyard, it is now a busy supply port for the modern oil and chemical industries. Its principal distinction, however, is a reconstruction of the Pont de Langlois, the bridge south of Arles (see box, p. 52) made famous by a painting by Van Gogh, which had been pulled down in 1926.

Marseille's limestone perimeter continues northwards with the Chaine de l'Etoile. Some 15km from the city, the **Château Gombert** has fine views and an interesting museum of Provençal art. The nearby **Loubière** caves can occupy an hour for enthusiasts of stalagmites and stalactites.

Allauch is an interesting town with no fewer than four 17th-century windmills on its elevated main street, offering views of the metropolis below.

For reminiscences of the days of Sahara forts and the pursuit of the Rifs, visit the Foreign Legion Museum next to their headquarters, just before the village of **Aubagne**, 16km east of Marseille.

Aubagne and its surrounding district has been swept to prominence by its association with the French film, *Jean de Florette* and its equally successful sequel, *Manon des Sources* (see p. 103).

*The Château d'If: prison for two counts,
Mirabeau and Monte Cristo*

The Mystery of the Magdalene

In AD46, tradition would have it that the Jews of Jerusalem resolved to rid themselves of the followers of Christ. They divested a fishing boat of its sail and oars, and cast out to sea Mary Magdalene, her sister Martha (see page 48) and her brother Lazarus, Mary Jacobe, Mary Salome, Sarah the servant-girl, St. Maximinus and Suedonius, the man born blind whose sight was given to him by Christ. This Boat of Bethany miraculously survived to reach Ste. Maries-de-la-Mer on the southern coast of France. Before separating, the party erected a small oratory to the Virgin Mary, where the two Marys and Sarah are thought to have been buried.

Meanwhile, it is said that Mary Magdalene and Lazarus furthered the cause of Christianity by preaching at Marseille in front of the Roman temple. This would have been a spectacular, public act of defiance in a Roman province by Christians previously involved in unrest at Jerusalem, and Mary Magdalene may well have been forced to take refuge in a cave on the northern face of the St. Baume Massif, some 25km north-west of Marseille.

Completely inaccessible in Roman times, now it can be reached by way of D2 through Gemanos, a series of hairpin beds to the Massif, then D80 to the pilgrims' hotel about 2km east of Plan-d'Aups. At the end of a steep path through the forest, the setting of the cave, whatever your personal beliefs, provides a powerful metaphysical experience, with its subdued lighting and relentlessly dripping water. Each 21st July, a candlelit mass takes place in the grotto, whose single dry spot, hollowed out as though by the pressure of a sleeping body, contains a recumbent statue of Mary Magdalene. When near death, the future Saint is said to have come down from her retreat to receive communion from St. Maximinus, at the spot marked by the Petit Pilon monument.

Again according to tradition, Mary Magdalene and later St. Maximinus were buried in the church crypt at what subsequently became St. Maximin-la-Ste. Baume, 32km to the north–east. In AD716, with the Saracens at the gates, the precious relics of the Magdalene and St. Maximinus were hidden by the Benedictine monks — rather too effectively, as they remained missing for centuries. But in 1279 Charles of Anjou, regent of Provence, discovered the lost tomb at St. Maximin, in a vault beneath a former Roman villa.

The Magdalene's body is said to have been remarkably preserved, but only part of the cranium survives at St. Maximin, contained in a 19th-century golden bronze reliquary in the crypt of the Basilica. The rest of her corpse was dismembered for the good and the great. Each of the eight popes that visited her shrine took away a small piece of her body, and other bones were dispersed among the royal households of Europe.

Jean de Florette

Jean de Florette and *Manon des Sources* were made in tandem by Claude Berri on location in the villages of Cuges-les-Pin and Sommières (see page 45) and in the Château de Renard, from the book by Marcel Pagnol, for many the most imaginative writer on rural life in Provence. Pagnol, the son of a Marseille school teacher, was born at Aubagne in 1905 but spent much of his life in the family home of La Bastide Neuve, which can still be seen at La Treille, a tiny village north–west of Aubagne, off the D44a. *Jean de Florette*, set in the Provence of the 1920s, recaptured many of his childhood memories of rural life that bordered on farce, but in an impossibly romantic and therefore wonderfully appealing manner. Jean of Florette, in fact the village of Cuges-les-Pin east of Aubagnes, is an unscrupulous peasant farmer. Played with almost inspired conviction by Yves Montand, he persuades his gullible nephew, an equally brilliant performance from Gerard Depardieu, to steal a spring, thereby setting off a chain of events in which comedy and tragedy are never far apart.

Marseille to Toulon

Five kilometres or so beyond the accepted limits of Marseille, defined perhaps by the gardens of the Château Borély, the summer motorist bent on sea breezes runs out of road. From here on the peninsula marking the end of the south bay of Marseille is dominated by the Marseilleveyre Massif. This limestone escarpment is suitable for sensible walkers, who can climb to **Montredon**, 432m above sea level, and be rewarded by magnificent views.

The Avenue Mazargues and the Chemin du Roi, together with back roads off D559 towards Cassis, lead towards the **Sormiou, Morgiou** and **Sugiton** *calanques*, deep water inlets finally accessible only on foot or by boat. They are like embryonic fjords, surrounded by towering cliffs.

At Cassis, a boat service runs from the Quai St. Pierre to even more delightful *calanques*, **Port Miou, Port-Pin** and **d'En Vau**; but as they are intended as round trips without a stop, you would have to negotiate with the boatman to be dropped off and picked up later in the day. If the boatman proves uncooperative, you could simply abandon the trip at the halfway point and walk back, as the journey from the more distant *calanque* still takes less than an hour. It begins with steep steps hewn out of the rock and turned into footholds through frequent use; the path then becomes difficult to find but eventually reaches the eastern end of Cassis itself. To start from Cassis, look for a sign '*calanques*', but note that the final descent into the inlets is more demanding, especially for young children. Of the three *calanques*, for families, the best choice is Port-Pin, an agreeable bathing spot shaded, as its name suggests, by hanging pines; for sheer scenery, d'En-Vau, a claustrophobic creek, twice the distance, squeezed between towering cliffs. You can drive to the closest *calanque*, Port Miou, complete with its strangely shaped, heather-clad rocks. To visit the others, however, do not be tempted to take the car: the closest point to these *calanques*, the car park at la Gardiole, off D559, is still at least an hour's walk away, and thefts from vehicles are common, as the thieves know that they can often work undisturbed for hours.

Cassis itself, producer of an outstanding white wine, is closed to cars. This lovely resort, on a semi-circular bay dominated by a backcloth of limestone hills, was probably one of the earliest coastal settlements of the Massalian Greeks; and the Romans, echoed in modern times, built luxury villas here. A stone quarry has existed in the nearby *calanque* of Port Miou for 2,000 years, supplying in turn the Greeks, the Romans, and the Genoans. By the 17th century, Cassis had settled into a comfortable existence as a fishing port and a summer refuge for the citizens of Marseille. Many fine houses survive from that period, as does the water festival, complete with jousting, to celebrate the feast day on 29th June of St. Peter, patron saint of fishermen.

However the true prosperity of Cassis dates from the middle of the 19th century. The building of the Suez Canal ensured that first-class stone was in great demand, and the village became fashionable throughout Provence thanks to the poem *Calendal,* published in 1867, by the region's great cultural crusader, Frédéric Mistral (see box, page 50).

For those continuing along the coast, avoid the dull, direct N559, strike south for the waterfront and, heading south–east, pick up the Corniche des Crêtes, the old D414A. This is not a route for inept drivers or anyone suffering from vertigo, as much of the road lacks barriers, and drops sheer into the sea. Ten kilometres out of Cassis stands Cap Canaille, the colossus of cliffs, 362m, the highest in France. The panorama is superb on a clear day.

Because of its obscure location, the ancient Provençal port of **la Ciotat** enjoyed a wide measure of autonomy down the centuries, until, in 1429, it achieved complete (if temporary) independence. To protect the deep-sea harbour, a small fort was built on the nearby **Île-Verte**, still an agreeable 30 minute trip by boat from the old port. However it was not until 1580, when much of the Marseille shipbuilding industry moved to la Ciotat to escape the plague, that the port became truly prosperous.

The dramatic cliffs close to la Ciotat, the **Cap d'Aigle**, have been the scene of two notable naval disasters. In the 3rd century BC a Roman freighter on its way to Massalia from Italy struck a rock and went straight to the bottom. Seventeen centuries later this Roman wreck was joined by the French auxiliary vessel, *La Corse*, torpedoed by a German submarine in January, 1918.

The town's resort is **la Ciotat-Plage**, 3km north-east, with a seafront of substantial hotels, splendid beaches, and exceptionally high levels of sunshine. The road continues to **les Lecques**, a quiet seaside town in a sweeping bay. To the south–east is the **Tauroentum Museum**, commemorating a Greek trading-post but built on later remains, those of a 1st-century Roman villa.

When it comes to climate, however, **Bandol**, to the south–east on D559, is supreme. Sheltered from the mistral by its wooded hills, and, less aesthetically, by its holiday apartment blocks, Bandol boasts a temperature ideal for palm and eucalyptus trees, scattered along its twin promenades, allées Jean-Moulin and Alfred-Vivien. They overlook three extensive beaches, each more than 450m long. The Plage Lido consists of pebbles, but the Plage du Renecros and the Plage du Casino have fine sand, ideal for children. Renecros is the most sheltered, and Casino the sunniest, in a resort that enjoys more than 300 days of sunshine every year. Its vines produce some of the best wine on the Mediterranean coast.

Easily reached by boat from Bandol, the island of **Bendor** is a holiday centre complete with a spurious but attractive Provençal harbour, a craft centre, nautical club, theatre and a museum housing 8,000 bottles of wines and spirits. The enterprise is the brainchild of Paul Ricard, the pastis millionaire, who bought the island in 1950. Ricard also purchased the Îles des Embiez, 7km south of Sanary, and turned one of them into a powerboat playground. Ten kilometres north of Bandol, near the fortified village of **le Castellet**, he opened the Paul Ricard motor racing circuit, regularly used for important events in the racing calendar.

Ollioules, inland via D11 from Sanary, has a Romanesque church and regular, vivacious flower-auctions, but is best known as the gateway to the **Gorge d'Ollioules**, through which the River Reppe once cut a path, but which is now dry, stony, and spectacular. On the sheer, volcanic rocks above stands the village of **Evenos** and its ruined castle keep, virtually deserted out of season, eerie by moonlight.

From the pink and white houses of Sanary, the coastline becomes the Cape Sicié Peninsula, a rich source of archaeological discoveries. The Greeks mined iron ore close to **Six-Fours-les-Plage**, at the centre of the peninsula, with magnificent views across the Bay of Toulon. Its Provençal romanesque church of Saint Pierre, probably dating from the 11th century with substantial 17th-century extensions, has beautiful decorations. The most notable is a 16th-century Madonna and Child in the choir, almost certainly by Jean Cordonnier, better known as Jean de Troyes.

This is the country of the *cromlechs*, great stone monuments or dolmens placed in a circle, sometimes with a flat stone on top, like those at the great British ritual site of Stonehenge. At **le Brusc**, on the tip of the peninsula, the stones pre-date the workings of copper mines by both the Greeks and the Romans.

Tamaris and **les Sablettes**, on the east coast of Cap Sicié, are two sandy, seaside resorts, with superb views of the Toulon roadstead. Pleasure boats run from Toulon in season. Tamaris, so called because of the abundance of locally grown tamarisks, has a harbour full of luxurious yachts. George Sand lived on the coast road between the two resorts and wrote her romance of *Tamaris* here in 1861.

The coast road rejoins the D559 at la Seyne, for the final run into Toulon.

9
Toulon, St. Tropez and Fréjus

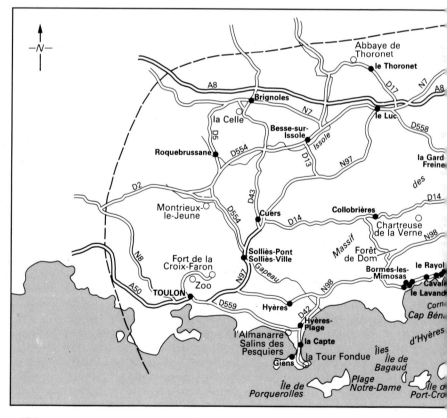

The most important naval base in France, with an outstanding natural harbour, Toulon's early income depended on a much more peaceful activity. At the waterline of the bay of Toulon could be found huge quantities of murex, a particular variety of mollusc that after intensive boiling produced a purple dye. What amounted to a Roman state dye works was established, making dye for the sumptuous purple robes worn by the Imperial family. After Rome disposed of its emperors, the manufacturers simply transferred their market to the Pope and his cardinals.

Toulon's pre-eminence as a naval centre was finally established by Cardinal Richelieu (1585–1642), who built an arsenal for the supply, refurbishment and repair of the French fleet. Many of the ships were galleys, whose benches were filled with Protestants and opponents of the monarchy, sometimes denounced anonymously without a shred of evidence. It was a measure of the brutal nature of the times that these wretches, chained hand and foot to their vessels, and forced to eat, sleep and relieve themselves where they sat, were a tourist attraction in the 17th century for visitors to Toulon. For a small consideration, the beat master would make the slaves row up and down the harbour, using his rawhide whip until they collapsed in exhaustion.

As the actual use at sea of these galleys declined, conditions on board were slightly relaxed. Slaves were allowed ashore in pairs, still chained together, and could earn money by playing or dancing. Incredibly, there were even a few volunteers, distinguished by the fact that they were allowed to keep their moustaches. Soon, however, the galleys gave way to shore-based prisons or transportation to the French colonies.

The galley slave lives on in the portal designed in 1656 by Puget for the old Hôtel de Ville. The strength and vitality of his unique marble masterpiece lies in the twin Atlases supporting the small central balcony. These Moslem figures are symbolic of the galley slave, bearing their full burden, their faces showing the strain and exhaustion of their timeless efforts. The portal has been restored to the quai Stalingrad but on an uninspiring modern building. It stands in front of the Naval Museum, which has models of famous ships and seascapes of famous battles. From the quai, guided boat tours of the *rade*, the huge natural waterway outside the harbour, leave at frequent intervals during the season.

In the centre of the Old Town, the Romanesque cathedral of Ste.-Marie-Majeure, whose 12th-century lines were ruined by 17th-century additions, is altogether a much too sombre

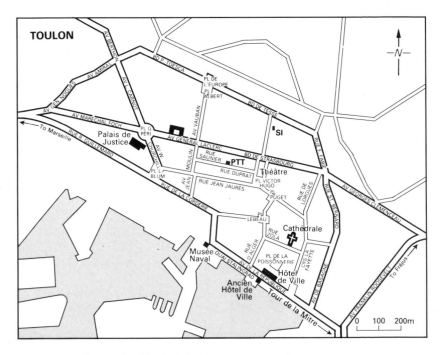

experience, despite its Classical 1696 façade.

North–west of the harbour, the congenial place Puget is worth more than a passing glance. At its centre is the 18th-century Fontaine des Trois Dauphins, designed by the architect Toscat and sculpted by Jean Chastel. Below and beside the cathedral, are two bustling markets: fish, appropriately, in place de la Poissonnerie; flower and vegetable, most days in cours Lafayette. Between here and the harbour some of the little streets of Old Toulon have been turned into an agreeable pedestrian zone, with smart boutiques and cafes. However, as you approach the waterfront, the atmosphere takes on a strictly nautical air around the rue d'Alger, with buzzing bars, lively girls and sailors celebrating shore leave, much as they must have done during Toulon's great maritime

era, not so long ago.

The best view of Toulon and its harbour on a clear day is from Mount Faron, a tall limestone ridge, 542m, from where even the biggest tankers look like bathtub toys. Just below the wooded summit, **Fort de la Croix-Faron** has a museum celebrating the liberation of Provence in general, and Toulon in particular, in August 1944. The round trip is 18km on D46. A funiculaire runs from upper Toulon almost to the summit, where there is a small zoo, stocked largely with harmless animals, ideal for children. Access by car is one-way only, on a narrow road with formidable bends.

To the north of Toulon, N97 leads to **Sollies-Ville**, an ancient village whose 12th-century Romanesque church was built on the foundations of a Roman temple. Its organ is one of the oldest surviving in France, made of carved walnut in 1499. The town is separated from **Sollies-Pont**, with its 17th-century château, by the winding river Gapeau, whose ascending valley with superb scenery runs north towards la Roquebrusanne beside the D554.

From Sollies, farther on N97, stop off in the Côte de Provence centre of **Cuers**, whose 16th-century church has a relic of St. Peter, mounted in gold. Or take D554 north–west, then D202 into a forest that conceals the twin ruined Cistercian monasteries of **Montrieux**. Montrieux-le-Vieux has almost disappeared; Montrieux-le-Jeune, founded in 1170, wrecked during the Revolution, was finally abandoned in 1901.

D554 continues north to **Brignoles**. Some 2km outside the town, on D405, only the ruined 13th-century chapter-house survives of the convent of **La Celle**. Its Benedictine nuns, alas, were ladies of easy virtue who plied their trade at the Court of the Anjou Counts, who established their winter palace (the summer was devoted to military campaigns) at Brignoles in the 13th century. The nuns' scandalous conduct eventually proved too much for Mother Church, and in 1660 the convent was dissolved.

In Brignoles, what remains of the Counts' unremarkable palace houses the *Musée du Pays Brignoles*. Its prize exhibit is the famous Sarcophagus of Gayole, transferred in 1890 from La Gayole, a hamlet with a ruined oratory, west of the town. At each edge of the façade of the Sarcophagus is a symbol of the old, heathen religion, Apollo on the left, Pluto on the right. But the central motifs show a fisherman, a woman in prayer, and a shepherd carrying a sheep across his shoulders. If

Baroque portal, Toulon's old town hall

the shepherd is indeed Christ as the Good Shepherd, the fisherman is symbolic of the fisherman of men, and the woman is seeking Paradise, then we have here a remarkable combination of Christian and pre-Christian imagery on a single tomb.

The nearby 15th-century Church of St.-Sauveur borrowed its Romanesque portal from the earlier Church of St.-Jean, when it was probably the palace chapel. An exceptional 15th-century carved door opens into the sacristy, which contains a 17th-century picture by Barthélemy Parrocet, the 'Descent from the Cross'.

In modern times Brignoles is known as a mining centre for bauxite, and as the distribution centre for many wines of Provence and the Var. You will ask in vain, however, for genuine 'Brignole plums', which nowadays come clandestinely from Digne in Haute-Provence. Brignole's own plum trees, all 185,000 of them, had been the basis of a vast dried plums industry, especially as sugar-plums; until they were destroyed in the 16th century by Catholic troops during the Wars of Religion.

South–east of Brignole, back down D554 and left on to D15, the former fortified town of **Besse-sur-Issole** stands on one of the few natural lakes in Provence, a haven for anglers. It is also just south of the N7, in earlier times the only road to the Riviera and Italy, a natural target for highwaymen. The Dick Turpin of 18th-century Provence was Gaspard de Besse (1756–81), whose life was as colourful as his costume, scarlet with silver buttons and buckles. His favourite haunt was the Auberge de Les Adrets, midway between Fréjus and Cannes, which still survives. Gaspard tended to linger longer with high-born ladies than

was strictly necessary for the purpose of divesting them of their valuables, and a few tears were no doubt quietly shed in 1781 when he was finally caught at another inn near Toulon, sentenced at Aix-en-Provence and broken on the wheel. For many years his head remained nailed to a tree on the Riviera road.

About 19km east of Toulon (via D559, D76 and D276) lies the resort of **Hyères**. Queen Victoria stayed in its suburb of Costebelle, which with its English church and line of luxurious hotels was almost an English preserve. But Victoria moved on to Cimiez and Hyères, almost overnight, ceased to be fashionable, leaving its wide avenues and lines of palm trees as a testimony to its former glory. Even its name sounds like the French word for yesterday, though its derivation is Latin.

Bormes-Les-Mimosas

By the 12th century the town was a bastion of the Knights Templar, whose Commandery or headquarters can be seen in the old quarter, full of steep narrow streets and enclosed gardens.

Today the ruins of the hilltop castle, demolished during the religious wars, accentuate the medieval atmosphere, particularly on market days, when the place Massillon has the same air of organised chaos it must have possessed in the Middle Ages.

Due south of Hyères and close to the sea, only the Romanesque chapel, St. Pierre-d'Almanarre, survives of a much larger Benedictine monastery. Fragments of Greek spears and pottery found nearby led archaeologists to uncover not one but two cities of the ancients, integrated with one another but of clearly defined separate periods. At the lower level, they found traces of the city walls, houses and latrines, probably from the Greek settlement of Olbia. At the higher level, probably from the later Roman city of Pomponiana, they discovered a statue to an early deity, a shrine, and the gateway leading to the harbour.

In Roman times the Giens peninsula was almost certainly still an island: it briefly became so again in 1811 when a great storm swept along the coast. The narrow strips attaching it to the mainland enclose a lagoon and the Pesquier saltpans, whose mounds of salt reflect the penetrating glare of the summer sun. In the east, they border a modern marina and the nondescript bathing beach of **Hyères-Plage**. Farther down the peninsula, a greatly superior beach serves the camping resort of **la Capte**, whose rows of tents look remarkably like the resting place of a medieval army. The elevated village of **Giens** lies amongst wooded foothills,

overlooked by a ruined château.

The Tour Fondu, on the south-east corner of the peninsula, was built by Cardinal Richelieu. Now it serves as the closest crossing point to the **Îles d'Hyères**. In the 16th century, plagued by Saracen raids, Francis I populated the islands with a collection of cut-throats and brigands, who were granted a pardon in return for promising to defend them against attack. Unable to eke a living from their barren soil, the criminals returned to their old way of life and became pirates themselves.

The largest of the group, **Porquerolles**, 8km long and just under 2km wide, is less than 20 minutes by ferry from the Giens peninsula. Its little port, built originally as a 19th-century military base, has rickety bicycles fo hire, the ideal way getting about this densely wooded island. The lighthouse on its southern coast cannot be visited but has a vantage point with wonderful views; the best beach lies to the north-east, the Plage Notre-Dame, a superb sweep of sand in a sheltered bay. Farther east, the island is restricted for military purposes.

Port Cros is a privately owned, rugged national park. The French government pays for its upkeep, and restrictions on camping, lighting fires, smoking (only permitted around Port Cros harbour, heavy smokers take note) fishing and game hunting are strictly enforced. However some of its flora and fauna cannot be seen elsewhere in Europe, and Solitude Valley, a ramble to the south coast, is a memorable experience. The island can be reached from Porquerolles, Hyères, Cavalaire, or, most easily, from le Lavandou. In each case the ferries pass between the **Île de Bagaud** — unin-

Ramatuelle at sunrise

habited, another national park with escorted visits only — and the ruined fortress of l'Estissac, built on the orders of Cardinal Richelieu in 1634.

In the 1920s the novelist D.H. Lawrence (1885–1930), suffering from a tuberculosis-related illness, came to Port Cros on his doctor's advice. He befriended a titled English lady whose pillow talk included the graphic description of her sexual experiences with a French farm worker. Lawrence used her confession as the basis for *Lady Chatterley's Lover*, for years banned in England as obscene and first published in Florence in 1928.

Most carnal thoughts disappear through sheer excess of flesh on the **Île de Levant**. Once inhabited by only a

Market at St. Tropez

few lighthouse keepers, this barren, unappetising rock became famous in the early 1930s as the Mediterranean's first nudist colony since ancient times. Quite why so many would-be nudists persist in visiting the place when they could disrobe quite happily on mainland beaches remains a mystery. It certainly cannot be the self-contained village of Heliopolis, complete with its own post office, hotel, and villas for rent on top of the cliff, where some of the estate agents enter into the spirit of things by stripping to a diminutive G-string called *le minimum. Voyeurs* should note that undressing is not compulsory but that cameras pointed in the wrong direction could result in the photographer returning topless and bottomless to le Lavandou.

East of Toulon, behind the resort of

le Lavandou, the village of **Bormes-les-Mimosas** perches like some pastel-coloured medieval amphitheatre, overlooking the sea, on a steep slope at the edge of the forest of Dom, where eucalyptus and mimosa abound. However visitors expecting a peaceful ambience should note that the nearby marina that serves the village has a capacity of 650 yachts. In the main square stands a statue of St. Francis of Paola, whose visit in 1481 coincided, fortuitously or not, with the end of an outbreak of plague. The 16th-century chapel of St. Francis contains a memorial to Jean-Charles Cazin (1841–1901), a notable landscape painter, who died at Bormes. Several of his works are on display in the town hall.

North of Bormes, via D41 and D14, visit **Collobrières**, a bustling little market town, with the river of the same name rushing between the houses, specialising in marron glacés, cork and handmade wooden Provençal furniture. From here, a signposted if bumpy track east leads to **Chartreuse de la Verne**, the ruins of a remote Carthusian monastery built c1170 in the epicentre of the Massif des Maures (see page 000). Standing in a wild and lonely landscape, on a plateau 414m above sea level, it was burned to the ground three times by the Saracens and finally became yet another victim of the French Revolution. However, enough survives to show that it was once an elegant and stimulating structure, particularly in its use of green serpentine stone to frame the cloister arcades. All around there are wonderful views of the Massif and the Verne Valley, a haven for dedicated walkers.

Le Lavandou, once a tiny fishing village, is now a thriving but relatively unfashionable resort, a mixture of high-rise apartments and terraced villas used almost exclusively as holiday homes. Its name, as one might expect, derives from the extensive lavender in the surrounding hills. Le Lavandou's heyday was in the late 19th century, when it was popular with artists and musicians, notably the composer Ernest Reyer (1823–1899), who lived and died in the town, and gave his name to a square next to the harbour-cum-yachting marina. From here ferries leave for the Île d'Hyères (see page 111).

Le Lavandou has a long, sandy beach, backed by a shady tree-lined promenade, though it becomes crowded in high season. There are better beaches for those who want more space to themselves to the east. The busy but scenic coast road, the Corniche des Maures (D559), passes half a dozen secluded resorts, **St. Clair**, **Aquebelle**, **Cavalière**, **Pramousquier**, **le Rayol**, **Canadel-sur-Mer** and **Cavalaire-sur-Mer**, each with a sandy beach and safe bathing. Cavalière's sheltered beach, backed by a delightful fringe of pines, is among the best in the Mediterranean.

West of le Lavandou, beyond **Cap Benat**, a rocky promontory 205m high with two 17th-century ruined castles and a lighthouse, much of the coast is barred to the public. Used as a military training ground, it leads to the official summer residence of President Mitterand.

In 1944 **St. Tropez** was reduced to rubble in house-to-house fighting between the Americans and the German garrison. Although rapidly rebuilt, for more than a decade St. Tropez, unlike the rest of the Riviera, simply stagnated. Then, almost overnight, its popularity was transformed by

Port Grimaud

the arrival in 1956 of Roger Vadim and Brigitte Bardot. Their circle of *glitterati*, which included Jean-Louis Trintignant, Annette Stroyberg, Sacha Distel, Fran-çoise Sagan, Gunther Sachs, Jane Fonda and Catherine Deneuve, was meat and drink to the press and fermented an adolescent sexual revolution. St. Trop, as it became known, was flooded with teenagers, who, à la Bardot, began taking off some and then all of their clothes on nearby beaches, occasionally pursued by dutiful gendarmes. Topless bathing, which began at St. Tropez in 1960, soon spread to the rest of the Riviera, further enhancing St. Tropez's reputation as an arbiter of progress if not always of taste.

As for the resort today, it is at once chic and passé, an amazing ambience that swings between the excruciatingly vulgar and the astonishingly vibrant. The most fashionable night club is the Cafe de Roi, outrageously priced, and the haunt of Jean Paul Belmondo and

Alain Delon. Le Bal and Papa Guy, slightly less expensive, are both patronised by Princess Stephanie of Monaco. The Café des Arts, in the Place Carnot, is the closest tourists can come to recreating the laissez-faire atmosphere of the sixties.

Unlike the rest of the Riviera, the resort has a well-defined season between May and October; as it faces north, St. Tropez can be rendered well-nigh uninhabitable by the mistral for much of the rest of the year. In season there are huge traffic jams in and out of the resort, which has one mediocre road, along which maniacal motorists leap-frog past one another. Parking is a nightmare as there is only one rather small car park, and tow trucks seem to work 24 hours a day. Whether through arrogance or sound commercial instinct, fewer shops and restaurants take credit cards in St. Tropez than in any other resort: this is a place to carry cash. However, nimble pickpockets

115

Le Thoronet

abound in summer, so this may well be a place where you do not carry cash for long. Although the cafés along the waterfront (in particular, Sénequier's) have the cachet and for male visitors offer a chance to ogle the nubile crew of the gin palaces moored in the harbour, their prices are breathtaking.

St. Tropez also has only one, rather grubby beach near the port. Its fashionable bathing places lie south-east of the town, accessible by car only from inland via the D93. You have to walk some way to use the free stretch of sand close to the **Plage des Salins**, the northernmost beach. The rest of the 7km stretch of glorious sand between the provocative **Plage de Tahiti** and the quieter **Plage de Pampelonne** is divided into 33 private sectors. The cognoscenti claim that Club 55, Moorea and la Voile Rouge are the most fashionable; they are also the most expensive, where a day out for two including sunbeds, umbrella, drinks and lunch by the sea could cost as much as a night at a luxury hotel.

The unofficial nudist beach, Blouch, is something of an irrelevance in that every beach is topless and most are bottomless for those with the cheek to carry it off. Keen students of anatomy will be amply rewarded for their investment, despite the occasional anachronism, such as an English lady in her sixties who every summer sells homemade cakes wearing nothing but a comprehensive tan.

St. Tropez first became famous in 1892, when the painter Paul Signac persuaded his little colony, fellow neo-Impressionists and a group of colourists called the Fauves, to join him there. Among them were Bonnard, Braque, Derain, Dufy, Seurat and perhaps the greatest, Henry Matisse, whose fine appreciation of design and superb balance of colour made him the acknowledged leader of this illustrious band.

Some of the best works by these artists have remained in St. Tropez, thanks largely to a local collector, Georges Grammont. To house them, in 1937 he bought the de-consecrated 16th-century chapel of L'Annonciade at the western side of the port. Matisse has three memorable works on display, 'Interior in Nice', 'Corsican Landscape', and the powerful 'Gipsy Girl'. Bonnard's 'Nude before the Fireplace' is an acknowledged masterpiece of Neo-Impressionist painting. The influence of the Fauves can be seen in the 'Landscape at l'Éstaque' by Braque, the 'Port of Boulogne' by Marquet, and St. Tropez's 'Place des Lices' by Camoin.

On 15th June each year the Fête des Espagnols, or *bravade*, celebrates the French defeat of 22 Spanish ships-of-the-line in 1637, with an armed procession that involves the simultaneous discharge of a score of ancient muskets. A much grander and more spectacular *bravade* takes place on 16th May, when more than 100 men dressed in 18th-century uniforms escort a bust of the patron saint in a procession around the town. The main parade takes place in the place de la Mairie, which is blackened by gunpowder from the constant firing of volleys of blanks into the ground.

St. Tropez's hinterland, called Presqu'île de St. Tropez, is a remarkable peninsula, rich in character and rural ambience. Sample it while you can, however, as its days are numbered. Property developers abound, making little attempt to blend apartments and villas into the existing landscapes. A striking example of misguided development can be found

Cathedral cloister, Fréjus

at **Gigaro**, once an exquisite tiny village on the south-west coast of the peninsula, now blighted beyond recovery.

Even the beautiful east-west coastal walk from La Bastide Blanche known as the *Sentier des Douaniers*, the Custom Officer's Path, a relic from earlier smuggling days, lives on borrowed time. All that prevents **La Bastide Blanche** from following disastrously in Gigaro's footsteps is the unmade, kamikaze road off the D93, so narrow that motorists determined enough to reach the settlement have scarcely enough room to turn around, let alone to park. Its sandy beach therefore remains largely tourist-free, which at weekends is more than can be said for

the **Plage de l'Escalet**, virtually the first free beach south of Port Grimaud.

Just inland of Gigaro, **la Croix-Valmer** is supposed to be the spot where Constantine the Great saw a flaming cross in the sky that indicated to him 'with this sign you will conquer'. A stone cross has been erected on the pass of la Croix, which Constantine is thought to have used on his way to Italy in 312 to defeat Emperor Maxentus. Constantine was influenced by the sign to convert to Christianity, and permitted freedom of worship throughout the Roman Empire.

Midway between St. Tropez and La Croix-Valmer (by D559 and D89), the ancient fortified village of **Gassin**, crowded with little houses, is perched high on a ridge — the perfect lookout point to ensure an early warning of the arrival by sea of Moors or pirates. Even higher are the nearby **Moulins de Paillas**, three ruined windmills together on a crest, difficult to find but with a most rewarding panorama of nearly 360 degrees, from the Mediterranean to the distant Alps. There is also a perfect view of the spectacular village of **Ramatuelle**, once a Roman outpost, and for 60 years (c994–1056) occupied by the Saracens. The winding alleys and little courtyards have a Moorish air, ideal shelter from the sun, and the fortified backs of its houses once served as an outer defence wall. Do not miss the great elm in the main square, place de l'Ormeau, which was planted as long ago as 1598.

St. Tropez is also the gateway to the **Massif des Maures**, one of the oldest land masses on earth, a vivid chain of grey, red and violet primeval rocks that

Overleaf: *Port Grimaud: marina in tranquillity*

119

covered much of the western Mediterranean, before the melting snows raised the level of the sea at the end of the Ice Age.

From 890 to 973 the Saracens were masters of the mountains and all who entered their domain. But in 972, when the Saracens kidnapped the Abbot of Cluny, Majolis, on his way back from Rome, William, Count of Arles, was sent by the Holy Roman Emperor to rescue him. He defeated the Saracens at what is now **la Garde-Freinet**, a village 20km north–west of St. Tropez, and ended their domination of the region. Despite its description as the Saracens' fortress, the ruined castle with its fine views, half an hour's walk north-east of the village, is of a slightly later period, and was not destroyed until the 16th century; it may have been built by Count William. He spared many Saracen prisoners, who, in return, taught his farmers how to roof their houses with the flat tiles still characteristic of the Provençal mas; to use the cork oak bark as bottle stoppers, and probably the secret of chestnut sweets known later as *marrons glacés*. The cork and the chestnuts remain the principal local industries.

The road to La Garde-Freinet passes through Grimaud, another ancient village that has given its name to the modern creation of **Port Grimaud** (see page 123).

Old **Grimaud** was probably another Saracen stronghold, and may have been taken at the same time as La Garde Freinet. In the 12th century the Knights Templar, who guarded the coast against the Moors, established a watch at Grimaud, which commands superb views over the Gulf of St. Tropez. Opposite the Romanesque church of St. Michel, which is first mentioned in 1096, is the Maison des Templiers, possibly built for the Templars in the 13th century. The 11th-century ruined castle became a Protestant stronghold in the 16th century, and was pulled down on the orders of Cardinal Richelieu. Grimaud confines visiting motorists to a car park slightly down the hill, so it is an extremely agreeable place to visit on foot.

The hot-bed of Provençal Protestantism was **Le Luc** to the north-west, designated under the Edict of Nantes as a town where they could freely practise their religion. In earlier Catholic times, it had a Romanesque church, of which only the hexagonal belltower survives, dating from 1517.

Le Thoronet, a charming but anonymous village, is reached by travelling east on N7 then north on D17. About 3km farther north-west stands the great Cistercian **Abbaye du Thoronet**, the oldest of the 'three sisters of Provence' — the others being Sénanque (see page 82) and Silvacane (page 78). The monks worked with remarkable energy, completing the most important buildings, including the church, the dormitory and the chapterhouse, in 15 years between 1160 and 1175. Its simplicity of style and perfect proportions, a reflection of the Cistercian concept of purity through austerity, was an evocative new art form that sets Le Thoronet above the rest. Its Romanesque two-storey cloister is also exceptional, as the east walk extends for some 36m, making it the largest cloister of its kind in Provence. The abbey has a defensive wall, which on its south side includes a small slab where the local population could leave their dead for the monks to give the body a Christian burial.

Port Grimaud, 6km west of St. Tropez with a connection by boat, takes its name from the nearby perched village of Grimaud (see page 122). Unclaimed marshland until 1964, it was created out of nothing by the Alsatian architect François Spoerry. Supposedly modelled on a medieval Provençal fishing port, it consists of a network of canals and Venetian bridges around a large, central lagoon. Its novelty value is an enormous tourist attraction, but the entrance to the resort is patrolled by uncompromising guards, so visiting motorists have to park outside; which is just as well, because the few roads are incapable of taking any significant traffic. Most of the houses, which are extremely narrow, have tiny gardens fronting the canals. Many are available for rent: the most attractive overlook the entrance to the harbour, where you can watch the smart yachts coming in or out, or back on to the beach, which is sandy, sheltered, safe and relatively quiet because of its inaccessibility to day trippers. Renting some kind of motor boat is essential to get the most out of the resort.

Ste.-Maxime, once a quiet fishing port, now concentrates its efforts on tourism. The shady, tree-lined promenade is an agreeable place to stroll, although the south-facing sandy beach can be extremely crowded in high season. Ste.-Maxime works hard to entertain its customers, with festivals, fetes and fairs throughout the summer, half a dozen nightclubs, a cinema and a casino. For those on self-catering, its vegetable market offers a huge range of cheap local produce. For those determined to eat out, the seafront restaurants are lively but scarcely a gourmet's mecca. The energetic holidaymaker can choose from water-skiing, wind-surfing, boating, cycling, golf and tennis. Serious yachtsmen complain that the marina is too small and much too congested in summer.

In front of the church, which has a notable 18th-century marble altarpiece, stands the Tour des Daumes, a square fortification built by monks from the Iles des Lérins (see page 132). The village, originally the Phoenician settlement of Calidianis, suffered severely in the Middle Ages at the hands of both Saracens and pirates, and appealed to the monks for assistance. They named the village after their patron saint, who is believed to have been the daughter of one of the Dukes of Grasse.

The rocky coastline between Ste.-Maxime and St. Aygulf has a number of tiny resorts, of which the most picturesque is **Les Issambres** with secluded sandy coves and up-market hotels.

St. Aygulf, just south of Fréjus, is a family resort, perhaps reflected most by the fact that its seaside shops seem to sell sturdier buckets and spades than elsewhere on the Riviera. Camping in luxury tents is very much the vogue. However, by Côte d'Azur standards, the prices reflect that many of its visitors are working to a budget.

Julius Caesar is popularly supposed to have founded what became modern **Fréjus**, as a military staging post, in 49BC. It became a major shipyard, and its harbour, created by dredging an existing lagoon, is believed to have spanned more than 50 acres, with over a mile of wharfs, quays, baths for returning sailors, workshops and even a laundry. The naval dockyard and arsenal spawned a population of nearly 30,000, not far short of the town's population today. The harbour was linked to the sea, which has receded by at least half a mile in the last 2,000 years, by way of a walled canal protected at its entrance by stone turrets. At night a huge submerged iron chain was winched above the surface to protect the harbour from surprise attack.

The end of the Roman civil war, and the long peace that followed, meant that Rome had little use for a large permanent navy and Fréjus went into gradual decline. Although the town survived the collapse of the Roman Empire, it was destroyed by the Saracens in the 10th century. According to at least one account, they were led directly to Fréjus by the so-called Lantern of Augustus, in fact a medieval hexagonal construction with a small pavilion roof protecting the torch, imposed upon the ruins of the Roman watchtowers. The Lantern of Augustus survives and can be reached south of the railway line via boulevard Decuers, then east along the southern defence rampart.

The Revolution finally put paid to Fréjus's aspirations as a maritime centre. The French King Henry II (1519–1559) had tried to use Fréjus as his principal naval base, but his sailors caught malaria from the mosquito-ridden marshes that had grown up close to the harbour due to centuries of neglect. The canal became progressively less navigable, and the whole area was put up for sale during the Revolution. The farmer who bought it filled in the harbour, and his heirs sold bits off to the railways.

Near the Porte des Gaules, now walled up but originally the gateway through the Roman ramparts, is the Roman amphitheatre. The best preserved of the ruins, though still badly damaged, it was probably built in the 2nd century AD. It measures 114m by 82m, and traces remain of the tiers of seats, some set into the hillside, that provided a capacity of around 10,000 spectators.

On the N7 towards Cannes, at the junction with the D37, stand two huge columns discovered on a Roman wreck at the bottom of the Gulf of St. Tropez in 1954. To the north–east can be seen traces of the Roman aqueduct that carried water to the town 42km from the river Siagnole. To maintain the flow, its arches, some of which are 18m high, brought the water along a conduit running beneath the parapet walk of the town ramparts, and from there direct into a water tower that formed part of the wall itself.

If the Roman ruins are disappointing when compared to those of Nîmes, Arles and Orange, there is ample compensation in its medieval church buildings. Started around 990 by Bishop Riculphe, they form a defensive square in the centre of the town. The small baptistery chapel, which dates from the late 4th century or the early 5th century, has a beautiful mosaic floor. The adjoining 13th-century Cathedral possesses a pair of outstanding Renaissance doors, dating from c1530, with eight coffered panels representing principally biblical scenes. At the entrance to the choir is a notable triptych representing St. Margaret surrounded by other saints, the work of Jacques Durandi, a master of the 16th-century Nice School that specialised in religious works. The 13th-century cloisters of Fréjus Cathedral, beautifully restored in 1925, lead out into a garden of oleanders and a central wall of uncertain origin. The delicate pillars of the cloisters support a superbly-carved 14th-century ceiling of wooden beams. Originally the cloisters had two complete storeys, but most of the upper level was destroyed during the French Revolution. Only the north gallery survives, leading to a small archaeological museum with Roman mosaics.

Nearly 2km south-east of Fréjus, the resort of **Fréjus-Plage** is the Benidorm of the Riviera. In summer thousands upon thousands of visitors are compressed into a narrow but seemingly endless strip of sand between the incessantly noisy coast road and the sea.

10
The Riviera:
St. Raphaël to Menton

By the strictest of interpretations, the true Riviera is as much Italian as French, describing the coast from Genoa to Ventimiglia in addition to Menton to Cannes. However, if the Riviera is judged by the longevity of its season, then it includes not simply the Côte d'Azur proper but also the Côte de l'Esterel between Napoule and St. Raphaël, the oldest resort of all.

St. Raphaël was a holiday centre for wealthy Roman families. On the site of the present rather inelegant casino, they built villas with sun terraces facing the sea, richly decorated with mosaics. The complex also had thermal baths, and a *vivarium*, a kind of fresh fish snack bar.

Unfortunately the villas did not survive the Dark Ages, and thereafter St. Raphaël disappears into complete obscurity until the end of the 18th century, when, on 9th October 1799, Napoléon landed in the harbour on his return from Egypt, an event appropriately commemorated by a pyramid in the avenue Commandant-Guilbaud. Although he had a hero's welcome, a few miles outside St. Raphaël his baggage coach was robbed, and Napoléon arrived in Paris penniless. Fifteen years elapsed before St. Raphaël saw Napoléon again, this time as a prisoner on his way to exile in Elba.

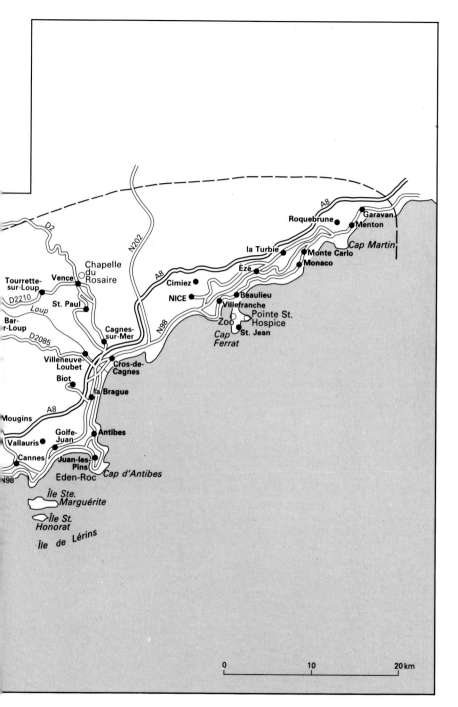

St. Raphaël might have remained an impoverished fishing village but for Jean Baptiste Karr (1808–90), the satirical novelist, who made it a fashionable watering-hole for Parisians. Karr abandoned Nice in favour of St. Raphaël as a winter home, building a villa here, entertaining the likes of Alexandre Dumas and Guy de Maupassant. You can get a taste of his lifestyle from the photographs displayed in the town's archaeological museum, also notable for its underwater discoveries, in rue des Templiers.

At **Valescure**, about 3km to the north, the British colony was large enough to justify a resident English chaplain in the 1890s: the large and faintly seedy hotels where British visitors spent the winter have been turned into apartments. St. Raphaël also has the distinction of being the first Riviera resort visited by Pablo Picasso, in 1919 (see page 134).

Today it is difficult to visualise what Karr and Picasso saw in St. Raphaël, for its erstwhile charm has been sacrificed to the demands of modern tourism. As a family resort with a long sandy beach gently sloping into the sea, guarded by the twin rocks called Lion de Mer and Lion de Terre, it satisfies a need for more moderate prices and less pressure to stay up until the small hours. But those seeking sensational night-life and the beautiful people must go elsewhere.

Between St. Raphaël and La Napoule-Plage are a number of tiny, undistinguished resorts. They include **Boulouris**, with its affluent villas and tiny harbour; **Agay**, a deep water anchorage used by the Greeks and the Romans; **Miramar**, with its private river marina, relaxed but apologetically elegant, uncertain of its identity; **Port-la-Galère**, a marina for the sailing fraternity unable to afford the mooring fees of Cannes or Antibes; and **Théoule-sur-Mer**, a thriving harbour in the 17th century, now with the dubious distinction of having almost certainly the only 18th-century battlemented soap factory to be turned into a private coastal château.

La Napoule-Plage, the sandy seaside suburb of the infinitely missable but villa renting centre of Mandelieu, has a genuine castle, overlooking the harbour and spectacularly floodlit after dark, 15th-century, with square towers that date back to the 14th. The troops of Savoy all but destroyed the castle in the 18th century. It was restored in the 1920s by Henry Clews (1876–1937), a rich American philanthropist and sculptor whose work, displayed in the château, possesses a breathtaking lack of talent.

Behind these tiny resorts stands the vividly coloured Esterel Massif, ancient volcanic rocks and ravines, once covered by a dense pine forest, alas, decimated beyond recovery in the great fire fanned by the mistral in 1964. The so-called direct route from Fréjus to la Napoule, the infamous N7, twists its way past **Mont Vinaigre**, reached by a forest track just short of the **Logis-de-Paris**, the N7's highest point. The view from the top towards the Mediterranean is simply superb.

The early history of **Cannes** seems to have been a succession of enforced bivouacs by invading armies. What with outbreaks of plague and incursions of pirates, it is little wonder that the 11th-century Tour du Suquet, built high above the old town, had its entry on the first floor accessible only by a ladder that could be pulled up when danger threatened.

Île Ste. Marguerite: prison of the Man in the Iron Mask

It was not until the fortuitous arrival of Lord Brougham in 1834 (see page 9) that Cannes became fashionable and eventually famous. His villa, on route de Fréjus, west of the town, has unfortunately been pulled down. However for most visitors, a stroll along his unintentional creation, la Croisette, is a memorable experience.

Waving gently in the sea breeze, its huge palms create 'a green twilight over the tables', just as they did for F. Scott Fitzgerald in his novel *Tender is the Night*. Almost exactly at the mid-point of this ostentatious affluence is the Hotel Carlton, built by the Swiss Henri Ruhl in 1902. Monsieur Ruhl came from Nice, where he was said to

The Cannes Film Festival

The Film Festival began in May, 1947 but became famous only in the 1950s, when producers realised that they could circumnavigate the influence of the Oscars, which celebrated films retrospectively, by promoting new pictures in Cannes.

The first attempt to introduce a mega-star was not, however, altogether successful. In 1952 Errol Flynn, anchored off Cannes in his yacht, was rowed ashore by his Jamaican crew in jet-black uniforms, serenaded by a calypso band. Unfortunately the effect was ruined by a Cannes lawyer who, no sooner had Flynn set foot upon French soil, served a writ. Flynn looked at it sadly, stepped back in the boat, and soon he and his yacht were a mere speck on the horizon.

Every year aspiring actresses try to outstrip one another to catch the eye of the media, giving the Festival a reputation for outrageous behaviour and shameless displays of affluence. Its entertainment remains lavish, though nothing has quite emulated the entire circus hired by the Americans to publicise *Around the World in 80 Days*, or the party given by the Greeks to promote *Never on Sunday*, where 1,000 guests did what is always done at a good Greek celebration, and smashed over 5,000 champagne glasses.

Ordinary visitors have little chance of meeting the stars or even seeing the films: all the tickets are distributed around the industry. Centred upon the Convention Centre between the harbour and la Croisette, the Festival is in fact the film industry's trade fair, where producers put together deals and resting actors hope to be remembered. The real stars come for as short a time as possible: Robert Redford was in Cannes for just two hours in 1988. Dirk Bogarde once observed that he never went to Cannes during the Festival because the town was always full of people that he had hoped were already dead.

be captivated by a local actress and courtesan, the half-gipsy Caroline Otero. When he was unable to persuade her to forsake Monte Carlo and Nice society, Henri Ruhl incorporated her most memorable feature into his stately pleasure dome at Cannes. The twin cupolas on the roof of the Carlton with their nippled spikes represent the breasts of La Belle Otero.

The bar of the Carlton remains the pinnacle of modern social activity. Although the hotel does not possess a garden, its private beach opposite provides a memorable lunch at a price

where one's instinct is to suggest that an extra zero has been added to the bill in error — an instinct, alas, wholly unfounded. There are other private beaches with slightly lower charges for sun beds and sunshades, and a surprisingly agreeable public beach at the east end of the town, close to a children's playground with a genteel circuit of mock antique motor cars.

The natural beauty of the town's surroundings combine with its effortless self-confidence to make this the supreme image of the Riviera, an image sustained since the 1920s. Then

The Man in the Iron Mask

The Île Sainte-Marguerite's most famous prisoner, The Man in the Iron Mask, is an intriguing mystery. Was he, as the French philosopher, Voltaire, claimed, the elder, disenfranchised brother of the Sun King, Louis XIV?

The prisoner died in the Bastille on November 19, 1703, after his transfer from Ste. Marguerite on September 18, 1698. The source of these exact dates is the second-in-command at the Bastille, Étienne du Jonquet, who records the new Governor, Monsieur de Saint-Mars, 'bringing with him in his litter a long-term prisoner who he had with him at Pignerol and whom he always keeps masked and whose name is never uttered'.

Unfortunately for the legend, in recording the death of the mysterious prisoner, du Jonquet undermines the existence of an *iron* mask. Of November 19, 1703, he wrote: 'The unknown prisoner always masked in a mask of black velvet died on this day.' This was his fourth and last domicile, but in every prison he had the same indefatigable jailer, Saint-Mars, a link that the 19th-century French historian, Theodore Iung, used to compile a list of every prisoner to pass through his hands. Only one could be traced to all four prisons where Saint-Mars served: Eustace Dauget.

By chance, the warrant issued by the Marquis du Louvois, Minister of War, on July 28, 1669, for the imprisonment of Dauget, has survived, and on it Dauget's name has been inserted, probably by Louvois himself, in the space left blank by his clerk. Minister and jailer corresponded regularly, more than 100 letters spread over 34 years. In them we find Saint-Mars reporting that the prisoner gives no trouble but accepts 'the will of the King'; and Louvois observing 'But as he is only a valet, he does not need a great deal'. It seems unlikely that Louvois was attempting to hide what he believed to be the prisoner's true status, as he subsequently allowed the Man in the Mask to take up such a role as valet to the disgraced Finance Minister, Nicholas Fouquet: an unthinkable breach of etiquette if the prisoner was of royal blood.

Whatever Dauget knew, it was sufficiently damaging for Saint-Mars to be ordered to kill him on the spot if he breathed a word about it, but only in the last resort: his death must be itself have been a damaging political secret. Otherwise the expense of altering the structure of no fewer than four different prisons to isolate his cell would never have been contemplated.

There seems only one plausible reason to continue to keep his face hidden: that in Paris, especially, his resemblance to the King would have been immediately noticed. It has also been suggested that Dauget posed an unthinkable double threat to the King: an elder brother who also knew that the King's mistress and mother of Louis' legitimised offspring, Madame de Montespan, was up to her neck in witchcraft. During his transfers from one prison to another, Dauget may have been locked in an iron mask.

On his death, Dauget's body was taken away in a sealed coffin, and everything linked to the prisoner was destroyed. His clothes, bed linen, blankets and mattress were burned; doors and window frames were removed; the tiles on his cell floor completely replaced; any metal items in his possession melted down. In this mystery the servants of the Sun King left no loose ends.

Antibes

as now, Cannes was never reticent at advertising its advantages, because

Menton's dowdy,
Monte's brass,
Nice is rowdy . . . but
Cannes is class!

Cannes may be, but the Municipal Casino in the Convention Centre certainly is not. The tables are franchised to temporary proprietors who set their own limit and frequently run out of money. On a recent New Year's Eve, one croupier was almost lynched by the gamblers when he called a halt to the proceedings after a winning streak against the Bank of eleven successful plays. The Palm-Beach Casino, a large white building on the Pointe de la Croisette, open during the summer, is much more sophisticated. It has a disco, swimming-pool, restaurant, and occasionally sparkling cabaret; jackets and ties for men, and dresses for the ladies, are compulsory.

From the east end of the harbour, boats ply back and forth to the wooded **Îles des Lérins**. The smaller of the two, **Île St. Honorat**, once had more than 7,000 monks and a religious library that was the envy of the Popes.

The larger and closer **Île Ste. Marguérite**, a monastic centre until the 17th century, was for a time the prison of the legendary Man in the Iron Mask (see page 131). His cell in Fort Royal, built by Cardinal Richelieu, can be visited.

Behind Cannes, the smart place to eat is **Mougins**, a perched village surrounded by extravagant villas and a formidable golf course. They provide a sharp contrast to the ancient village houses that almost touch one another at the first or second floor above its winding, claustrophobic streets. Mougins was once larger than Cannes and proudly independent, defended by ramparts and a fortified 14th-century gateway, which still survive. Now the only invaders are hungry diners, who make for the little square with its wedge of restaurants, their appetite whetted by the long walk from the car park. Motor vehicles are not permitted in the centre, and woe betide any foreigner who tries to elude the village female Flying Squad on little motor-bikes.

North-east of Cannes, the small

town of **Vallauris** takes its name from the Latin *Vallis Aurea* or 'golden valley', after the orange and mimosa groves, bestowed upon it by the Romans. Its thriving pottery industry, with more than 100 master potters plying their wares, dates back to the time of Emperor Tiberius (AD14−37), when brick-fired kilns were already active. The pottery also has an Italian influence, the result of immigration by Genoese families in 1501. However its real stimulus was provided by Pablo Picasso (see page 134), who lived here for part of each year between 1947 and 1954 and created a studio. The town has a Picasso bronze, 'Man and Sheep', in the main square in front of

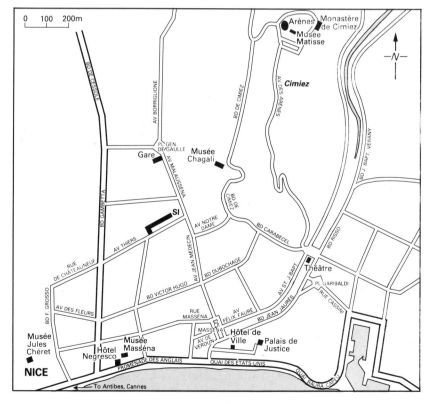

Pablo Picasso

It is open to debate whether Picasso or his friend Henri Matisse had the greatest influence on 20th-century art. Picasso moved restlessly through the creative medium. Quite apart from the extraordinary range of his canvases, he designed stage sets; experimented for a year in a ceramics studio at Vallauris; dabbled in sculpture; tried his hand at lithography; and illustrated translations of classical texts. Together with the French painter, Georges Braque (1882–1963), Picasso undermined the concept of central perspective, the foundation of most art for more than five centuries. In its place they introduced Cubism, a means of creating a three-dimensional image on a flat surface without the use of perspective. To Cubism Picasso added *collage*, in which paper, string, wood and wire became to him as important a medium as paint itself.

Picasso was as inexhaustible as he was creative, producing over 80 years more than 10,000 separate works of art. He seems to have lived a life hovering on the edge of inspired madness, grotesquely anti-social and decadent, a cultural renegade, and according to accounts by his intimates, systematically degrading for the women who loved him. Picasso's last wife shot herself; one of his mistresses hanged herself and another went mad.

the church. He also gave Vallauris 'War and Peace', strictly not a mural as it is painted on plywood screwed to the wall of the Picasso Museum; the museum is housed in the medieval chapel.

Vallauris runs south into **Golfe-Juan**, a thriving, sheltered marina and resort, whose principal distinction is the fact that most of its beaches, unlike the rest of the Riviera, are entirely free. A plaque on the quayside commemorates Napoleon's return here from Elba on 1 March, 1815.

The name **Antibes**, a Greek settlement in the 6th century BC, is derived from *Antipolis*, meaning 'the city opposite', presumably opposite to Nice, at the other end of the *Baie des Anges*. Following the discovery in the harbour wall of the Stone of Terpon, with its phallic shape and an inscription extolling the physical rewards of love, there is a serious suggestion that Antibes was

an early sailor's retreat, little more than a seaside bordello. Later, it became just a dilapidated frontier outpost, successively fortified and flattened by the armies of the French King and the Emperor. The impecunious Alexandre Grimaldi sold Antibes to France in 1608, whereupon its fortifications were strengthened first by Vauban and later by Colbert: particularly the Baroque Fort Carre, the core of an eight-pointed defensive star that has survived to house the town's impressive archaeological museum.

The castle of the Grimaldis, built on the foundations of the Roman castrum and dating back to the 14th century, was loaned to Picasso (see also page 128) as a studio in 1946. He worked there between August and November, producing a prolific series of large scale works on eccentric materials inspired as much by post-war shortages as a creative urge. The best is probably 'Joie de Vivre', satyrs and centaurs in the classical tradition, assembled in fibro-cement over 9ft in length. It can be seen where Picasso painted it, in what is now called the Musée Picasso, because in gratitude of the hospitality given him by the town, Picasso left them virtually his entire output of this period, together with his ceramics produced at nearby Vallauris (see page 133).

The best night-life is not in Antibes itself but three miles north at **La Brague**, where the Siesta club allows anything but that. In the daytime it is a dynamic lido, with water sports that other lidos have not yet invented, a supervised adventure playground for children, and dog kennels complete with dining facilities. Even the design of the casino cleverly encapsulates a breaking wave in its concrete structure. At night the club offers a kind of perpetual *son-et-lumière*, with musical floodlit waterfalls and dark caverns lit by inextinguishable torches.

Just inland, the little village of **Biot** combines an arcaded, floral charm with a formidable reputation as the centre of two industries, Provençal glassware and terracotta ceramics. Its potential in ceramics attracted Fernand Léger (1881–1955), the painter who had abandoned abstract art to become the celebrated interpreter of the factory age. Unluckily for Biot, Léger died within weeks of buying a large studio in the village; but it was turned by his widow into a museum of his works.

South of Antibes, the true wealth of the Riviera manifests itself on the peninsula of **Cap d'Antibes**, full of luxury apartments and even more luxurious and secluded villas. At the very tip is the hotel Eden Roc, the cele-brated mecca of the stars between the Wars, when an American literary colony turned the coast between Antibes and Juan-les-Pins (see page 11) into the Riviera's first summer playground.

Juan-les-Pins, on the western edge of the Cape, is strictly a summer resort, monopolised by young and unsophisti-cated visitors. Its little streets are honeycombed with bars, restaurants and shops that have to cater for a clien-tèle with far more energy than money.

There are sandy beaches east of Antibes, but so crowded in summer that the tourists lie cheek by jowl soaking up the sun. In the much quieter 1920s, Pablo Picasso (1881–1973) (see box) set the pattern here that was to last most of his life: sleeping late, a swim in the sea, lunch on the beach with friends, then working frantically from early afternoon until far into the night.

Nice, settled by the Greeks and the Romans, survived through the cen-turies because of its natural defensive position and a dogged determination to play off the Counts of Provence, its liege lord, against the warring families of Italy, the Guelphs and the Ghibel-lines. The solution, to become part of the independent middle kingdom of Savoy in 1388, proved a disastrous miscalculation, despite the construc-tion of a formidable fortress over-looking the harbour. Nice simply became a battleground of the great powers, and even its great fortress was finally taken and destroyed in the 18th century, during the War of the Spanish Succession. Now vulnerable to attack, Nice went out of its way to welcome influential and creative visitors, includ-ing the Dutch painter, Louis Van Loo; and the Duke of York, brother of King George III, in 1764, followed by the

The Negresco in Nice, one of Europe's great hotels

entire family of the Duke of Glou-
cester. By 1787, 115 foreign families,
most of them ailing British with pneu-
monary complaints, had taken up
winter residence.

The French Revolutionary Wars
prevented further foreign visits, and
Nice was occupied by French troops,
among them in 1794 the young
Napoléon, in lodgings at what is now
No. 6, rue Napoléon. He returned in
1796, this time as commander desig-
nate of the French army in Italy, and
lived in much grander surroundings in
the rue St.-François-de-Paule, by the
opera house. In the Musée Massena,
housed in a palace near the sea, is a
collection of furniture and artefacts of
the Empire period.

Although a raised promenade had
been started beneath the demolished

citadel about 1750, much of the sea
front consisted of a rough track inter-
spersed with trees, an ideal hiding
place for thieves and beggars. The
Anglican clergyman Lewis Way persuaded the local British community that
they could eliminate this nuisance in a
most Christian fashion. Many of the
poorer families in Nice had been
stricken by the failure of the orange
harvest, so they were put to work on
enlarging and paving the path, until it
stretched over 10km and became,
because of its benefactors, the Promenade des Anglais.

Savoy used Nice as a bargaining
pawn in the great chess game of

*The pedestrian zone and antiques market,
Nice*

Renoir

Pierre Auguste Renoir (1841–1919), one of the greatest artists of his age, was born in Limoges, where he began modestly in trade as a painter on porcelain. Later he earned his living as a portrait painter before discovering his true metier with the Impressionists. Renoir came to Haut-de-Cagnes in 1895, but found his first house, in the centre of the village, too small and moved in 1903 to les Collettes, on the edge of Cagnes-Ville. Already suffering from arthritis, this was the period when he painted in vivid colours — red, orange and gold — often nudes in sunlight. Increasingly crippled, he was compelled to paint from a wheelchair after 1909, and near the end his brushes had to be tied to his fingers.

The wheelchair sits with a poignant emptiness in Renoir's studio, left just as it was when he died, with his walking sticks, easel, coat and cravat. Disappointing, his studio contains only one of his canvases but many souvenirs of his family and companions, including Gabriel, his children's nanny, cook, nursemaid and favourite model.

Europe, and in 1860 ceded the town to France.

The coming of the railway in 1864 transformed the prosperity of Nice, as royalty made it Europe's winter capital. The visitors included Czar Alexander II, King Leopold of Belgium, Queen Victoria (see page 10) and King Ludwig of Bavaria who, sent packing by his subjects, became a founder member of the Nice Carnival Committee. The annual carnival, still celebrated during the fortnight before Lent, is a lavish affair of floats, flowers and fireworks.

The old Roman suburb of Cimiez took on a new lease of life, with the building of grand palatial hotels to accommodate Europe's upper-classes, such as the Grand, the Alhambra, the Winter Palace and, finest of all, the Excelsior Regina Palace. They have become, through due passage of time, apartment blocks, clinics, and an expensive old people's home.

Sun, sand and sea were still considered unnecessary until the turn of the century, when the absence of waterfront hotels provided an opportunity for two young entrepreneurs, Henri Ruhl and Henri Negresco. After an unrequited love affair, Ruhl went off to open the Carlton at Cannes (see page 30), then, on the strength of his success, returned to launch the Hotel Ruhl at Nice in 1905.

Negresco hired the Parisian architect, Eduard Niermans, who had been responsible for the Moulin Rouge in Pigalle, to build an even more splendid hotel, but unfortunately it was not completed until 1912. During the First World War and in its immediate aftermath, the hotel was badly damaged and its wealthy clientèle remained at home. The Rumanian-born Negresco, who had begun his career as a gipsy violinist playing to hotel diners, went bankrupt and died in Paris in 1920.

After several periods of uncertainty, exacerbated by its reluctance ever to question the resources of its regular guests, the Negresco has survived. Its page-boys, clad in their red breeches and dazzling white gloves, still greet visitors with studied deference. The royal saloon has a great chandelier made for the Czar; the Aubusson carpet is quite simply the best that money can buy. Every bedroom suite is decorated to reflect a different period of French style: including Napoléon III, Empire and Louis XV. On the walls are original works of art by such as Cocteau and Picasso. The public toilets on the ground floor look like some replica of a salon in the Palace of Versailles.

All that mars a stay of nostalgic luxury at the Negresco is the dull but constant noise of traffic, midway along the Promenade des Anglais, a race-track with no chequered flag, perilous to cross even at traffic lights. In pleasant

St. Paul de Vence

Grasse

Villefranche, the port where the cruise ships anchor

contrast, the streets around rue Massena are now a pedestrian zone, full of shoppers by day and patrons of open-air cafes at night.

However the true heart of Nice lies between the sea and the empty château hill, still worth a visit for the view. Around cours Saleya, the centre of Savoyan Nice, a vegetable and flower market operates every day, from eight till noon, later if business is brisk. To the north the grid of streets disintegrates into a random maze of alleyways and steps, a paradise for pasta-lovers, as almost every known variety is an offer here. We could be in the back streets of Genoa or Naples, so authentic seems the Italian atmosphere. The bistros and bars are full of artists, putting off the moment when they have to start work.

At the lower end of Cimiez, once the fashionable suburb of Nice, is a museum dedicated to the works of Marc Chagall (1889–1986), the Russian artist whose flights of ingenious fantasy are said to have inspired Guillaume Apollinaire to create the concept of 'surrealism'. Chagall, an Orthodox Jew, studied at St. Petersburg and Paris, where he developed his technique of huge canvases scattered with bold, dramatic concepts and colours. He lived at St. Paul-de-Vence, west of Nice, from 1949 until his death.

Cimiez, to the north, has excavated its early Roman settlement. Although the remains cannot compare with those of western Provence, they include part of the 3rd-century Roman baths, a tiny amphitheatre, and a piece of masonry distinguished only by its size, said to have belonged to the original Temple of Apollo.

The upper storey of the Villa des Arènes is dedicated to the works of the painter Henri Matisse, who opened a studio in the nearby Regina Palace Hotel in 1938, and lived in Cimiez until his death in 1954. The collection spans his entire career, and is particularly interesting in that it includes the preparatory sketches of some of his most important works, including 'La Danse'. Matisse is buried in the cemetery of the nearby Franciscan monastery.

East of Nice by the N7 or A7, **Cagnes** is the generic name for three distinctive communities, that improve in direct proportion to their distance from the sea. First, and worst, is the sprawling seaside resort of **Cros-de-Cagnes**, whose unique combination of urbanised motorway, high-rise apartments and seething supermarkets has destroyed all traces of the original fishing village. The scale and tastelessness of the building development has almost engulfed what was once a chic race-track, the Hippodrome.

Second, the supremely mediocre and insufferably noisy commercial centre of **Cagnes-Ville**, relieved only by its Renoir Museum (see box, page 138).

Third, the rocky heights of **Haut-de-Cagnes**, a medieval village dominated by its castle of the Grimaldis, who ruled here from 1309 until the French Revolution. Rainier I began its construction early in the 14th century, but its true beauty derives from Henri Grimaldi, who in 1620 turned it into an elegant château. He devised its best feature, an imaginative triangular inner courtyard, and commissioned the Italian frescoes in the ceiling in the grand hall. The most dramatic, the 'Fall of Phaeton', the first chauffeur in history to be murdered, as his incompetence provoked Zeus to kill him with a

Monaco

The Principality of Monaco owes its continued existence to the prolific fertility of the Grimaldis, who in 1333 embraced no fewer than 110 male descendants. With the exception of Cannes and Nice, a Grimaldi ruled in every Riviera town at some time or other between the 10th and 16th centuries. The Principality and the Prince came together in 1309, when Francesco Grimaldi purchased the rock from the Genoese.

The Monegasques, though, have stubbornly resisted the idea of taxation throughout their history, and the pocket principality was practically bankrupt when François Blanc inherited the concession at an ailing Monte Carlo casino in 1863. Blanc's success was helped by the abolition of gambling in Bad-Homburg; and by the fact that the frustrated aristocrats could switch easily to Monaco on the new Riviera railway.

As for Charles Deville Wells, the man who became the hero of the famous song, *The Man Who Broke the Bank at Monte Carlo*, he arrived at the casino in July 1891, with £4,000, the profits of a series of swindles back in England. Although his maximum winnings on any given day at the casino were £10,000, his reckless play established his reputation. In 1892 Wells broke the bank five times, but the bank eventually broke him; and at the end of the year Wells was arrested at le Havre and duly sentenced to eight years hard labour at the Old Bailey in London for a further catalogue of frauds.

Monte Carlo Casino, rebuilt in 1878 by Charles Garnier, architect of the Paris Opera, no longer has the charisma of earlier times, despite its sumptuous decor. Most visitors (who must show their passport) are restricted to the public rooms, where evening dress is certainly not required, and gambling is confined, Las Vegas style, to batteries of slot machines.

High above the harbour, the Prince's Palace, open only in the absence of Prince Rainier, dates from the 13th century, although its Italian Renaissance rooms are predominantly of the 15th century. The millionaires' yachts in the bay below, and the million dollar pearls in the night clubs, confirm that Monte Carlo is still an irresistible magnet for the jet setters who own their means of transport.

thunderbolt, is by the Genoese artist J.B. Carlone. Its trick of perspective is so ingenious that visitors instinctively duck, convinced that Phaeton, horses and chariot are about to come crashing to the castle floor instead of their mythological destination in the River Po.

The castle also contains the Museum of Mediterranean Art, of which it must be said that the title is superior to the collection. However,

appropriately placed in the boudoir of a lascivious and, it is said, licentious Marquise de Grimaldi, is an unusual twist: 40 portraits of the same artist's model, Suzanne Solidor, a cabaret singer who gave generously of her services to such artists as Dufy and Cocteau.

Haut-de-Cagnes became a fashionable rendezvous for artists after the arrival in 1895 of Renoir.

'The Cheese', the famous casino at Monte Carlo

From the three faces of Cagnes, the road turns up into the hills towards **Grasse**, favoured winter residence of Queen Victoria (see page 10). Grasse, with Provence, ultimately became part of France, which was the key to a new, and flourishing perfume industry. Hitherto Grasse had made its money through buying ships and cargoes (at one point it owned Marseille's entire trading fleet) and the production of leather goods. Now it found a French market for perfumed gloves among the Medici family, who brought the idea from Italy. Within a century the sideline had become the principal industry of Grasse, the manufacturers even opening shops in Paris to market their goods. Marie Antoinette wore some of the products of a Grasse perfumier,

Fargeon, on her way to the scaffold.

The principal raw materials of scent are perfume flowers, especially wild mimosa, but also roses, jasmine and violets. However many more exotic substances are added during the process, including musk from Tibet, canine civet from Ethiopia, vanilla from the West Indies, ginger from India, aniseed from Spain, patchouli oil from Iran, sandalwood from the Solomon Islands, and the rather less exotic whale vomit. At the risk of huge over-simplification, the secret of Grasse perfumes is in mixing alcohol with the antique oils.

You can hear a more detailed explanation by going on a tour of the Fragonard perfume factory and museum. However there is no 'hard sell' and Fragonard perfumes, otherwise sold mainly wholesale, cannot be bought as cheaply elsewhere.

Fragonard is the most famous name in Grasse because of Jean-Honoré Fragonard (1732–1806), son of a poor tanner, who became the painter to the royal Court. His brilliant technique and vivid colours enabled him to produce scenes of Court life and magnificent landscapes that anticipated the great Impressionist painters.

The winding, climbing streets of old Grasse remain largely intact, though the Grand Hotel where Queen Victoria stayed has gone, and so has her other residence, the Villa Rothschild, leaving a space occupied in summer by hundreds of campers. The best views to be found in this Victorian health resort are from the 17th-century cours Honoré-Cresp, near the perfume factory, a promenade with an uninterrupted sight-line of the sea.

Just south of Grasse, there are two villages worth a detour on the D9. **Pegomas**, on the river Siagne, is surrounded by wild mimosa; **Auribeau**, its medieval houses clustered around the square and 18th-century church, lies north-west of Pegomas via D509 and overlooks the lush river valley.

North of Grasse, perched like an eagle's nest over the Gorges de Loup, is the castle of **Gourdon**. A formidable obstacle in the 13th century, built on Roman and Saracen foundations, it was pulled down in the 16th century and given a terrace garden by Le Nôtre. The views from the road just below the village, a plunging panorama of rugged ravines, are breathtaking for those without even a suspicion of vertigo.

The **Gorges de Loup** are at their most spectacular during the autumn, when the russet colours compete with the swelling rivers, and whirling waterfalls drop sheer into the earth.

Just to the south, **le-Bar-sur-Loup**'s gothic church of St.-Jacques was built in the second half of the 15th century. It has two unusual features, a solitary side aisle, and a 15th-century painting on an oak panel known as the 'Danse Macabre'. It shows five couples in courtly attire performing the tambourin, a classical dance of Provence, menaced by Death as a skeleton bowman whose arrows have just accounted for a man and a woman. Three more devils are fully occupied in gathering up the souls of the recently departed. The origin of the painting may be a contemporary Lent ball given by the Count of Bar, which ended in disarray when several guests were stricken with a virulent plague and died as they danced.

Tourrette-sur-Loup, slightly north–east, takes its name from the three fortified towers that strengthened the natural defence line of houses high above the valley. Most of those houses have been turned on a suffocating scale into craft shops, especially for local ceramics.

The most photogenic feature of **Vence**, 10km from the sea behind Cagnes, is place de Peyra, believed to be the site of the Roman forum, with a splendid fountain sculpted in 1822 and a spreading chestnut tree.

To the north, off D2210, lies the **Chapelle du Rosaire**, created by Henri Matisse between 1949 and 1951. The great painter designed everything — walls, ceiling, floors, doors, windows, the altar, the vestments, even the lighting.

D.H. Lawrence died at Vence in 1930; so, too, in 1986, did the painter Marc Chagall, whose works are included in a remarkable exhibition at **St. Paul-de-Vence**, 5km south. In the Hotel Colombe d'Or is probably the greatest private collection of modern art anywhere in France. It includes paintings by Bonnard, Derain, Dufy, Léger, Matisse, Mirò, Picasso and Vlaminck, many of which were accepted by the owner, Paul Roux, in lieu of payment for board and lodging by the artist. 'It was,' said Picasso, 'my kind of hotel: no name outside, no concierge, no reception, no room service, and no bill.' When Roux died in 1954, his collection was already worth millions and his hotel the haunt of celebrities, indeed virtually the permanent home of Yves Montand and Simone Signoret. Nowadays room service is provided, and everyone gets a bill; indeed it is impossible to see the art collection without staying in the hotel or eating in the restaurant, not a choice for those with an view to economy.

It was perhaps the increasing inaccessibility of Roux's collection that encouraged the Paris art dealer and publishers, Aimé and Marguerite Maeght, to create the Fondation Maeght, a museum of modern art, standing in parkland outside the village. Its exhibits are changed at least three times every year, apart from some permanent mosaics by Chagall and some ceramic sculptures by Mirò.

The cobbled streets of St. Paul are perhaps unique in that most of them date precisely from 1537, the year Francis I pulled down more than 600 houses and the old city walls to create the great ramparts and towers that still exist today. The alleys and steps, paved with pink mosaics climbing past picturesque squares with little fountains, are remarkably well preserved, despite sieges by the Piedmontese and occupation by the Austrians. The 12th-century Romanesque parish church has a wonderful interior, including a nave with three aisles so broad that they form almost a perfect square.

North-east of Nice, the wooded bay of **Villefranche** owes its name to the tax exemptions promised to the local inhabitants by Charles II of Anjou, who wanted a secure deep-water harbour for a fleet to preserve his communications with Sicily. Its 14th-century chapel of Saint-Pierre was decorated, not altogether successfully, by the poet and playwright Jean Cocteau in 1957.

St. Jean, a lively little fishing village with bars and bistros catering for insomniacs, lies in the eastern corner of the affuent peninsula of **Cap Ferrat**. Determined walkers can find a way through to the Points St-Hospice and be rewarded with brilliant views of the whole Mediterranean coastline; but most of the peninsula is rocky and has been bought up by villa owners jealous of their privacy. Only one can be visited: the villa once owned by Beatrice Ephrussi, sister of the millionaire banker Baron Edouard de Rothschild, designed to accommodate her collection of French and Italian art, but whose charm lies principally in its exotic setting and ornamental gardens.

Somerset Maugham lived on Cap Ferrat at the Villa Mauresque and savaged one luckless tourist who, unwittingly as it happens, ventured on to his lawn. 'This is not a zoo,' said Maugham, 'and I am not a monkey in a cage.' It seems slightly ironic to observe that nowadays there is indeed a zoo, built on the site of a drained lake that once formed part of the estate of King Leopold II of Belgium, the Villa les Cedres. If the zoo's chimpanzees seem slightly overweight, it is because they eat party tea six times a day in summer for the benefit of the tourists.

The Corniche Inférieure, or Lower Corniche, begun in 1863 and completed in 1878, continues to the languidly sophisticated resort of **Beaulieu**, sheltered from the vagaries of the mistral, though not noted for its throbbing night life. Its heyday was in Victorian times, when aristocrats built grand villas and exotic gardens, many of which survive, unfortunately not open to the public. But on a small peninsula high above the Mediterranean stands the Villa Kerylos, Beaulieu's greatest attraction for visitors. It was constructed between 1902 and 1910 by the archaeologist Theodore Reinach, and is the perfect recreation of a classical Greek villa. Reinach lived here for 20 years, and used the finest materials, including Carrara marble, to match his formidable collection of genuine antiquities.

Beyond the Principality of Monaco (see box) lies the luxuriant resort of **Menton**, protected on three sides by sharply rising mountains, with a climate favourable enough to ensure constantly ripening lemons, still the heart of Menton's prosperity. Menton was a tiny Monegasque fishing village in 1860 when three events transformed its future. Menton was annexed by France; it was placed on the route for the prospective Riviera railway; and Dr Henry Bennet wrote a travel book for ailing consumptives recommending its climate. By the turn of the century, Menton had 5,000 British inhabitants, with their own church, club, newspaper and library. You can see their names in the 19th-century cemetery, laid out on the site of the old citadel. Below, the largely 12th-century baroque Church of St-Michael has obvious Italian influence. So has the Musée-Regionale in the rue Larchey, notable for its famous skull of the prehistoric 'Grimaldi man'.

To the east of the old quarter, with its stepped alleyways and 17th-century Italianate houses, the smart suburb of Garavan was once the home of Katherine Mansfield, in the Villa Isola Bella. The Spanish novelist, Vicente Blasco Ibañez, author of *The Four Horsemen of the Apocalypse*, spent his final years in exile at the Villa Fontana Rosa. Particularly worth a visit is the Villa les Colombières, designed and built by the multi-talented Ferdinand Bac around the turn of the century. Bac, who claimed to be the great-nephew of Napoléon Bonaparte, was a comic writer and architect-gardener. The Greco-Roman style of the villa contrasts vividly with the tiered perspective of the gardens. Both, however, are typical of Menton: nostalgic grandeur and echoes of past glory.

On the Corniche Moyenne (Middle Corniche), built between 1910 and 1928 to relieve congestion on the lower Corniche Inférieure, a superlative panorama rewards the energetic visitor to **Èze**, 1,550 ft above the sea. A Ligurian stronghold, it was probably occupied by the Romans and the Saracens, though no positive evidence survives. Its medieval houses blend so perfectly with the rocky outcrop that they seem part of the pinnacle itself, occupied by tourist termites clambering around its corkscrew alleyways from dawn to dusk. Louis XIV demolished the last of its fortresses in 1706, leaving a wild cactus garden which decorates the summit.

The Corniche Supérieure (Upper Corniche), built by Napoléon in 1806,

Menton, end of the French Riviera

follows closely the route of the ancient *Via Aurelia* which ran from the valley of the Rhône all the way to Rome. Augustus provided the impetus for this original great all-weather highway, and it was probably he, at 480m above the sea, who erected the great Trophy of the Alps at **La Turbie**. It commemorated the final subjugation of the guerrilla Ligurians who had ambushed Roman convoys and even careless Roman legions: 44 conquered tribes were listed at the base of the monument, which was originally 50m high, 38m wide, with a 20ft statue of Emperor Augustus surveying the apex of the Roman world. St. Honoratus did his best to demolish what he believed to be a pagan structure; it was later used as a quarry and turned into a

citadel; and finally blown up during the War of the Spanish Succession. However an American philanthropist, Edward Tuck, financed its partial reconstruction by Camille Formige, whose work was completed by his son Jules in 1934.

The hillside village of **Roquebrune** has a largely 13th-century keep. Along with the narrow winding streets, it provides a perfect cross-section of feudal society, for whose peasants at Roquebrune life began literally at the bottom.

Below Roquebrune the exclusive peninsula of **Cap Martin**, once deserted, owed its initial impetus in the 19th century to the Empresses of Austria and France, Eugénie and Elisabeth, who patronised the Hotel du

Cap Martin on its very tip. It was a favoured haunt of Winston Churchill, of the author, J.B. Yeats, who died here in 1939, and the architect Le Corbusier, who was drowned while swimming in a high sea off the Cape in 1965.

11
Inland Provence

Haute Provence lives up to its title: take any large scale map of the region and you will find sparse green valleys nestling between range after range of grey, menacing mountains. In medieval times, the menace was real enough. In the Montagne d'Albion, east of Mont Ventoux and west of the much fiercer Mountains of the Lure plateau, the D63 leads north of the sleepy village of **Ferrassières**. About 3km and several hairpin bends later, it crosses the **Col de l'Homme Mort**. The origin of the name remains obscure: but then dead men tell no tales.

Forcalquier, an insignificant market town today, was once the thriving independent capital of this region, whose Counts and Countesses tried to better themselves in the 13th century by marrying into the principal nobility of Provence. In doing so they lost their capital to the Counts of Provence, who enlarged the former Cathedral of Notre-Dame, and turned the town into a major artistic centre.

Christianity preceded the Counts by several centuries. Take D12 and N96 towards Sisteron, and make a small diversion on D101 to the ruined abbey of **St. Donat**, thought to have been founded in the 6th century by the hermit monk, St. Donatus. The French Government has given a grant towards

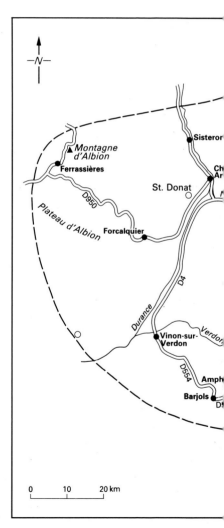

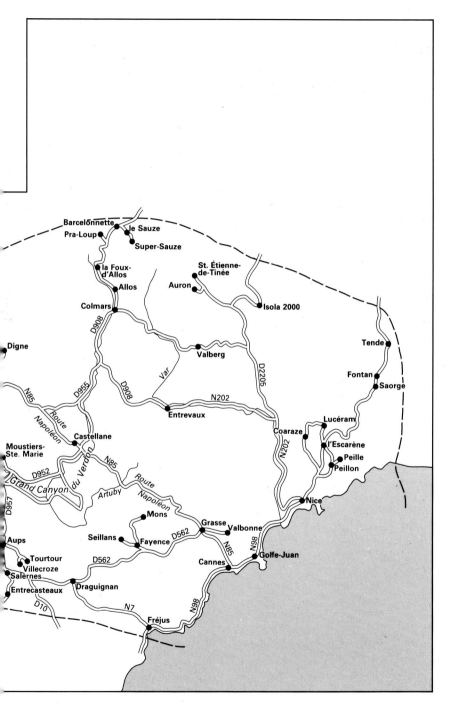

the restoration of its abbey church, an acknowledgement of its significance as an outstanding example of early Romanesque architecture.

Sisteron, a resort centre on the narrows of the Durance, was the natural gateway to Provence and once a town of great strategic importance. The ramparts of its citadel rock were reinforced in the 16th century by Jean Erard, engineer to Henry IV. Unfortunately, the town was heavily bombed during the Second World War, and only a few of its clustered alleyways and tiny squares have survived. In one of them, at No 20 rue Saunerie, is the house where Napoléon had breakfast on 15th March 1815, on his return from Elba on what became known as the Route Napoléon (see box, page 154).

The arrival of Napoléon during a storm, on a mud-splattered mule, was perhaps the most exciting moment in the history of **Digne**, a thermal resort with shaded and faded boulevards, where Victor Hugo set the opening chapters of his epic novel *Les Misérables*.

To the north-east, **Colmars** received the attention of the more famous military engineer Vauban, who linked its twin medieval castles, the Fort de Savoire and the Fort de France, with massive 17th-century fortifications. The ramparts have largely survived, but Colmars has lost all signs of belligerence. It is a popular summer resort, with a series of pedestrian precincts, little squares leading into little squares, each with a cooling fountain.

The fortifying of Colmars was due to its strategic importance at the old frontier between Provence and the domain

Moustiers-Ste. Marie, village beneath the rocks

The Route Napoléon in Provence

After landing at Golfe-Juan on 1st March 1815, on his return from Elba, and receiving a scant welcome at Cannes, Napoléon marched north towards Paris and on 2nd March reached Grasse, where he was given provisions but very little else. As the main roads were barred by troops loyal to the French King, Napoléon took the bold gamble of using the back roads to Sisteron through St. Vallier and Castellane, even though in doing so he had to abandon his cannon and his coach. He passed through Digne and Sisteron without opposition, and at Grenoble the garrison flocked to his banner.

of the Duke of Savoy. In the 14th century, the Duke annexed **Allos**, now the centre of a winter resort for experienced skiers and après-skiers; the mountain pass of the **Col d'Allos**, closed in winter and a hair-raising experience even for the best drivers in summer; and the Barcelonnette valley.

Barcelonnette is what it sounds, 'little Barcelona'. Indeed until the 18th century it was called Barcelone, a reference to the fact that like much of Provence, it once owed fealty to the Counts of Barcelona. Nowadays, it is almost little Mexico, as the town participated in Spanish emigration to Central America in the 19th century, and Mexican goods are still displayed almost as though they are local produce. Some Barcelonnette families made their fortune in Mexico and returned to scatter the valley with Mexican haciendas.

The northernmost town of Provence, hemmed in by mountains, Barcelonnette is an ideal centre from which to visit the ski resorts of **le Sauze** and **Super-Sauze**, in addition to **la Foux-d'Allos**. As most skiing enthusiasts seem to think nothing of a four- or five-hour transfer to the resort of their choice, they are all within reach of

Nice Airport. However, there are more sophisticated resorts much closer to Nice in the Alpes-Maritimes, of which the best are Valberg, Auron and Isola 2000. **Valberg**, outstanding for beginners, is close enough to bathe in the Mediterranean and ski on the same day. **Auron** is much more in the grand manner, a plateau surrounded by higher peaks, with quality hotels and a vigorous supply of evening entertainment. **Isola 2000**, the newest of the major ski centres, is an interconnecting complex that looks rather like a moon base that has strayed from its orbit; not a destination likely to find favour with unenthusiastic skiers in the party.

Provence remains the place of perched villages, that stretch from the Rhône valley to the Alps like a string of pearls, an overworked metaphor perhaps, but it describes them so perfectly. In all there are close on 100, improvised bastions against the marauders from the sea, little houses huddled together in concentric circles, sometimes built around a citadel, where, with true medieval inequality, their liege-lord slept the most secure.

If you can only visit one, visit the supremely spectacular **Saorge**, reached from Nice using D2204 and A204. As you pass through the **Gorges de Saorge**, the village suddenly looms up to the right, seemingly defying gravity as it clings to the mountainside. No road, however steep, could reach it from here; and in fact you have to travel on to the next village of Fontan to find a way. Saorge itself is closed to cars, and best seen from the terrace of the Franciscan church on its eastern outskirts, a perfectly preserved crescent of pink and grey houses, many 17th-century and some 15th-century in origin.

There is more memorable scenery in the flaming rocks of the **Gorges de Bergue** north of Fontan, worth a diversion if only to marvel at the feat of engineering that produced the adjoining pre-war Nice to Turin railway. Blown up in 1940 to frustrate an Italian

invasion, the line was only re-opened in 1980. Its most extraordinary feature is the spiral of tunnels inside the mountain, where the train appears and reappears at different levels.

North of the Gorges, on N204, is **Tende**, almost on the border with Italy, and a good base for excursions. Built in tiers on the mountainside, it is overlooked by the ruins of the Château des Lascaris. The Church of Notre Dame-de-l'Assomption dates back to the late 15th/early 16th centuries.

On the same route from Nice, take a turning north off D2204 at l'Escarène, the D2566. It leads directly to **Lucéram**, whose stepped Italianate houses, a reminder of the time when it was owned by one of the Italian princes, are jumbled together in an evident anxiety to leave no opening for the Saracen invader. The ornate church of

Tende: on the steep slopes of the Alpes-Maritimes

Gorges de Verdun

remorselessly to **Peille**, whose medieval houses and 13th-century church gaze out upon terraced vineyards too steep for tractors and tilled by hand just as they were centuries ago. By retracing the hairpin route, D21 continues south close to the equally compelling village of **Peillon**, on a sharp pinnacle of rock. The enthusiasm of rich Niçois for a weekend retreat has sapped its peasant roots, but at least their houses have been painstakingly preserved.

One of the most fascinating of all the perched villages, much farther to the west, is also among the most obscure. First go to Draguignan, northwest on N7 from Fréjus, then to northwest to Salernes, via D557 and D560. Thirteen kilometres (via D560 and D32) to the west is **Fox-Amphoux**, a tiny hamlet with a superb hotel (see page 172) in its medieval square; hardly any other inhabitants; and a patchwork quilt of a history. People lived on this wooded hill in the Bronze Age; the Romans fortified it; the 11th-century church was built by the Knights Templar, who settled at Fox after losing their Mediterranean lands to the Turks. The Revolutionary Paul Barras, sent to the Convention as deputy for Nice, built a small château here. It was probably the influence of Barras that enabled Fox-Amphoux to keep its fine church bell, when Napoléon ordered every bell in France to be melted down to make cannons.

Ste. Marguerite belies the village's turbulent past, as in the 15th century Ludovico Brea made this a prolific centre of religious painting, of which the most distinguished example is the retable of Ste. Marguerite behind the high altar. The beauty of the village has been partially spoilt by a forest fire in 1986 which left it isolated in a charred landscape and licked the outer walls of the houses.

Even closer to Nice, this time leaving D2204 earlier on D15, the crested village of **Coaraze** has a series of intricate vaults and arches designed to protect the route to its summit from the blazing sun. Its main square has two sundials of vivid enamel, a local speciality and prosperous cottage industry.

South from l'Escarène, D21 takes a left turn into the D53, a series of perpendicular twists and bends climbing

South of Salernes is a village for once in a valley, **Entrecasteaux**, with a quaint humpbacked bridge and Gothic church, but dominated by its formidable 17th-century château. This ruined

The perched village of Castellane

castle was rescued in 1974 by Ian McGarvie-Munn, a Scotsman who had made his fortune in India, and is kept open by his children. As a family home, entry is by way of the modern kitchen.

North of Salernes is **Aups**, tourist and truffles centre at the foot of the Montagne des Espiguières. South-east of Aups, the skyline stops at **Tourtour**, a village with a vast panorama across the foothills of Provence, a ruined château and an equally derelict medieval fortress.

North of Aups, the spectacular village of **Moustiers-Ste.-Marie** at the foot of a deep ravine is divided by a mountain torrent, the Rioul, and the Maire. Suspended over the valley is an iron chain 227m in length with a gilded star at its central point, said to have been placed there by Baron Blacas in the 13th century, in fulfilment of a vow he made during a long captivity at the end of the Seventh Crusade. In the 17th century Moustiers acquired the secret of faïence pottery from an Italian monk, and the industry has intermittently flourished, although many of its modern products are of uncertain quality.

Unfortunately, the questionable reputation of its pottery and its magnificent setting have made Moustiers an intolerable magnet for tourists, and like Fontaine-de-Vaucluse and les Baux, it is best visited soon after dawn or shortly before sunset.

The problem is exacerbated because Moustiers-Ste.-Marie is also an ideal departure point for the **Grand Canyon du Verdon**, the deepest canyon in Europe, 762m deep and almost 21km in length. A tour by car should be made in the clockwise direction, keeping the Canyon on your right, where the views are superior and parking is easier. The best viewpoint is on the south side at the **Balcons de la Mescla**, just past the Pont de l'Artuby, at the confluence of the Verdon and Artuby Canyons, a dizzy panorama straight down into the depths. On the north side, from another splendid viewpoint called the **Pont Sublime**, a footpath winds it way on a series of cliff ledges above the Canyon and through a series of tunnels. Anyone contemplating this trip should be in first-class physical condition, have a good head for heights, warm clothing, climbing boots and a torch; and have at least eight hours to spare. The bed of the canyon and the river Verdon can be navigated in canoes, but only with an official guide.

East of Moustiers and north-east of Castellane, **Entrevaux** is another of that comparative rarity in Provence, a medieval village not on a mountain top. But this frontier outpost on the old border with Savoy had little need of elevation after 1695, when Louis XIV's chief engineer, Vauban, rebuilt its ramparts to complement its natural defences of the turbulent river Var. They survive almost intact, giving Entrevaux almost a Disneylike appearance, with superb views of the Alps from its lofty citadel.

From the Grand Canyon of Verdon the string of pearls stretches to Grasse and southwards to the criss-cross alleyways of medieval Valbonne. For epic views, go north of Fayence to the little village of **Mons**, full of hidden courtyards linked by steep steps and tiny alleyways. Then south to **Seillans**, whose fountains cascade tier upon tier, and whose 12th-century château once resisted the Saracens. Not altogether surprisingly as *seillans* is the Provençal word for a pot of boiling oil.

12
Practical Information

The most popular likely arrival points of visitors to Provence and the Côte d'Azur are:

    Avignon — by motorway, motorail, train, TGV or air
    Fréjus — by motorway or motorail
    Nice — by motorway, motorail, train, TGV or air
    Marseille — by train, TGV or air

Most of the recommended routes begin at one of these points, with supplementary tours of the hinterland, the Camargue from Arles, and the area around the major tourist centre of Aix-en-Provence.

Travellers should note that opening dates and times of hotels and restaurants are a decision for individual proprietors who can — and do — make alterations from year to year. Opening times for places of interest are also subject to frequent alteration.

How to Get There

By Air: Nice and Marseille are major international airports: Nice-Côte d'Azur airport is 7km south-west of the city, an easy taxi ride, and with a helicopter link to Monaco/Monte Carlo; Marignane Airport is 28km north-west of Marseille, just off the A7 motorway, and with a rail connection to the city centre. Avignon–Caumont airport is 8km south-east of the city.

Discounts: The French Government does not encourage charter flights, and unlike other Mediterranean destinations, there are very few cheap fares or cheap package holidays. However, Air Inter has a *Carte Evasion* which offers savings for anyone planning the equivalent of two round-trips or more from Paris to Provence. Air Inter also offers substantial discounts to travellers under 26 and senior citizens.

Tel: Air France (Marseille) 91.54.92.92, (Nice) 93.96.31.51 or 93.50.59.34, (London) 01-499-9511.

British Airways (London) 01-897-4000, (Marseille) 91.90.77.10, (Nice) 93.83.19.61.
Air Inter (Marseille) 91.54.77.21, (Nice) 93.31.55.55.

By Air and Rail: French Railways and Air France offer an inclusive arrangement using Air France from various UK airports. The price of the ticket is less than taking the entire journey by rail. Contact Air France or travel agents.

By Rail: British Rail offer connecting services with French Railways from London Victoria using the Sealink ferry service between Folkestone and Boulogne, but you have to change stations in Paris, from the Gare du Nord to the Gare de Lyon. A daily sleeper service operates between Calais and Nice, all the year round. The *Train à Grand Vitesse* (TGV) from Paris Gare de Lyon, with speeds up to 270kph, takes 4hr 40min to Marseille and 7hr to Nice. There are slower overnight services from Paris with convenient stops between Avignon and Nice all along the Côte d'Azur. Passengers picking up entirely domestic services should take care to *compostez*, that is, to date stamp their ticket in a machine provided at the entrance to the platforms, or risk a heavy fine.

Discounts: The Eurail Pass offers young travellers residing outside Europe unlimited trips for 1–2 months on French Railways. The France Vacances pass entitles anyone residing outside France to discount travel on French Railways for up to 30 days. There are also discounts for senior citizens, family groups, children aged 4–10 (half price), while children under 4 travel free.

By Motorail: French Railways offer regular motorail services from Calais, Boulogne and Dieppe to the South of France. Dieppe has a ferry connection from Newhaven, near Brighton; Boulogne and Calais shorter connections from Folkestone and Dover by ferry or hovercraft.

Information from French Railways, in the UK, (London) 01-409-3518; in the USA, (Beverly Hills) (213) 272 7967, (Chicago) (312) 427 8691, (New York) (212) 582 2816, San Francisco (415) 982 1993, Coral Gables (305) 445 8648.

By Car: From Calais, Marseille is attainable, barring any major roadworks, in under 10 hours, Nice in less than 13. Traffic jams out of Paris on the autoroute A6 are common on Friday nights throughout the year, and on Saturday mornings in summer. Particular days to avoid are the first and third Saturdays in July, and the first Saturday in August, the start of French holidays, when long queues and multiple accidents are common. The weekends of 14th and 31st July, 15th and 31st August can be equally trying for the return journey. Motorway tolls are expensive, but credit cards are accepted for payment.

Renting Cars: French Railways offer an inclusive car–train and Air France an inclusive fly–drive package at several destinations in Provence. The prices of the major companies are under-cut by local firms, but the vehicles may not be as well maintained and should be carefully checked, especially the jack and spare tyre. Local firms may also be less willing to provide immediate replacement vehicles in the event of breakdown. Central reservation numbers ((1) indicates a Paris number):

Avis (1) 45.40.32.31
Europcar (1) 30.43.82.82
Hertz (1) 47.88.51.51

Many companies now require drivers to be 25 or over and almost all refuse to accept drivers under 21. An international driving licence is not required.

Insurance: The so-called reciprocal medical insurance between EEC countries can prove impossibly bureaucratic, duplicates cover on other still essential holiday insurance and, in France, only provides for up to 75 per cent refunds in any event. The best advice is to disregard it completely. Comprehensive insurance, covering all medical emergencies and, where appropriate, problems with a vehicle, is obtainable from Europ Assistance in the UK on (Croydon) 01-680 1234, or in the USA from World Wide Services (Washington) (202) 429 0655. The international green card which confirms 'foreign use extension' of a domestic motor car insurance is still the most acceptable proof of valid insurance.

Passports: UK full and British Visitors passports are accepted in France without visas. US citizens must obtain a visa at a French consulate in the USA, either by personal application or by post.

When to Go

Provence and the Côte d'Azur have a very long season when good weather can be anticipated, but never guaranteed. The best months are usually July and August, with unrelenting sunshine, but they are also the most crowded. The Riviera winters are extremely mild. On the coast, the average temperature in January and February is still 13°C, and in the height of summer, over 27°C, with a mid-summer sea temperature of between 20 and 23°C. However, inland summer temperatures may be paralysingly hot, and there is virtually no rain, a reminder that Provence is, in effect, simply the northern edge of the Sahara desert. Inland winter temperatures are also extreme, with snow covering the hills and mountains. Sun and sea bathing are agreeable on the Riviera coast even in late autumn, but be prepared for sudden, violent storms. In early spring, especially, the fierce and unpleasant wind known as the mistral can blow for days on end.

Where to Stay

Hotels: Provence has more luxury hotels than any other area outside Paris. The best offer superb accommodation, food and service, with prices to match. However, within all but the most luxurious hotels, the quality of rooms can also vary tremendously. Except for a brief stay, a superior room in a modest hotel may prove more acceptable than an inferior room in an expensive hotel. When booking, check the amenities: most hotels now provide showers en suite, but not all provide baths and WCs. Many hotels now ask for either an *arrhes* (deposit) or an *acompte* (payment on account), or for the number of your credit card in advance. Hotels prefer credit cards in the Visa/Barclaycard or Eurocard/Mastercharge/Access groups to such charge cards as American Express or Diners' Club.

At Christmas, Easter and between mid-June and late September, and on most other Friday and Saturday nights, forward reservations in Provence are essential. On shorter stays, you are expected to eat dinner in most hotels on at least one night. Most hotels offer reduced rates on longer stays for *pension complète* (room, breakfast, lunch and dinner) or for *demi-pension* (room, breakfast, and a choice each day of lunch or dinner). Increasingly the same charge is made whether the room is occupied by one or two persons. Many hotels offer family rooms in which small children can be accommodated on extra beds.

Hotel chains are prominent in Provence and are particularly useful for touring holidays by car, as their hotels are often located on the outskirts of towns. The reservation numbers of the principal chains are ((1) refers to Paris numbers):

Ibis	(1) 60.77.93.20
Inter-Hotel	61.73.40.63
Mercure	(1) 60.77.93.20
Meridien	(1) 42.56.01.01
Novotel	(1) 60.77.93.00
Sofitel	(1) 60.77.65.65

For more original hotels, often in a rural setting, usually individually owned but jointly marketed:

Logis et Auberges de France	(1) 43.59.91.99
Relais du Silence	76.98.35.79
Relais et Châteaux	(1) 47.42.00.20

Self-catering: This is extremely popular in Provence, and the properties available range from modest apartments or cottages to grand villas complete with staff. However, the prices of many are hugely inflated. Ideally, the rental company should deal direct with both owner and client, should take the property for the whole season, and should have a local representative able to sort out any problems. Additionally, the owner or local caretaker should be responsible for any necessary repairs. One of the very few companies that meets all these criteria, and has properties over a wide rural area of Provence and the Côte d'Azur, is Vacances en Campagne, of Bignor, West Sussex RH20 1QD, UK (07987 344 or 366). For more modest rural properties in Provence rented direct from the owner, contact the Fédération Nationale des Gîtes Ruraux de France in Paris (1) 47.42.25.43.

Shopping Hours

With the exception of major department stores, shops tend to close for at least two hours between 12.00 and 3.30, opening at 8.00am or earlier and closing sometimes as late as 8.00pm, except on Saturdays, to compensate. Food shops may open from 7.00am to 1pm and close altogether in the afternoons. They also open on Sunday mornings. Except in major Riviera resorts, very few other shops open on Sundays and some may also remain closed on Monday mornings. Markets begin at 7am or 8am and end shortly after midday; go early for the best produce and late for the odd bargain.

Telephone

The international code for France is 33. For calls to the UK from France, dial 19, wait for the second tone, then 44, then the UK number (omitting the first 0). For calls to the USA (except Alaska and Hawaii) from France, dial 19 then 1, then the US number, including the area code.

Discounts: Reduced rate calls to the UK are available at 50 per cent discount between 9.30pm and 8am (French time) on weekdays, on weekends after 2pm on Saturdays, and on public holidays. Reduced rates to the USA are available 10pm to 10am weekdays and Saturday, and all day Sunday. An increasing number of public telephones accept only the *Telecarte*, where you buy units in advance on a card obtainable from post offices and shops.

Emergencies: Police, dial 17. Fire, dial 18. Ambulance services are regional, usually with the first two figures common to all local numbers, then 67.00.00. To report passports or related problems, ring the consulate in Marseille (UK) 91.53.43.32 or 91.37.66.95, (US) 91.54.92.000. To report lost or stolen credit cards, ring:

American Express	(1) 47.08.31.21
Barclaycard/Carte Bleue/Visa	(1) 42.77.11.90
Diners' Club	(1) 47.62.75.75
Eurocard/Master Charge/Access	(1) 43.23.46.46

National Holidays

1st January, Easter Monday, 1st and 8th May, Ascension Day, Whit Monday, 14th July, 15th August, 15th November, 25th December.

Time

France is one hour ahead of UK time, except for about one month from mid-September when France reverts to GMT + 1 and British Summer Time remains in force.

Banking Hours

Banks are universally closed on Sundays, national holidays, local holidays and lunchtimes, which can be as short as 12.00–1.30, or as long as 11.15–3.00. They may open as early as 8.05am and close as late as 5.55pm. In provincial areas, they are as likely to be open Tuesday to Saturday as Monday to Friday. The only solution is to go and see.

Conversion Tables

km	miles	km	miles	km	miles
1	0.62	8	4.97	40	24.86
2	1.24	9	5.59	50	31.07
3	1.86	10	6.21	60	37.28
4	2.48	15	9.32	70	43.50
5	3.11	20	12.43	80	49.71
6	3.73	25	15.53	90	55.93
7	4.35	30	18.64	100	62.14

m	ft	m	ft	m	ft
100	328	600	1,968	1,500	4,921
200	656	700	2,296	2,000	6,562
300	984	800	2,625	2,500	8,202
400	1,313	900	2,953	3,000	9,842
500	1,640	1,000	3,281	3,500	11,483

ha	acres	ha	acres	ha	acres
1	2.5	10	25	100	247
2	5	25	62	150	370
5	12	50	124	200	494

kg	lbs	kg	lbs
1	2.2	6	13.2
2	4.4	7	15.4
3	6.6	8	17.6
4	8.8	9	19.8
5	11.0	10	22.0

°C	°F	°C	°F	°C	°F
0	32	12	54	24	75
2	36	14	57	26	79
4	39	16	61	28	82
6	43	18	64	30	86
8	46	20	68	32	90
10	50	22	72	34	93

Town Guides

Aigues-Mortes
Information: pl St.-Louis (66.53.73.00).
Opening Times: Constance Tower and Ramparts, Apr–Sep 9–12, 2–6; Oct–Mar 10–12, 2–5.
Hotel: Les Remparts, 6 pl d'Armes (66.53.82.77). 18 rooms. Converted 18th-century house just inside town walls, period furniture, fine restaurant (closed Mon out of season) but forget the children. Hotel closed Nov to mid-Mar.
Restaurant: La Camargue, 19 rue de la République (66.53.86.88). 17th-century stone house, huge candlelit suppers, gipsy guitarists and, more often than not, Manitas de Plata (playing) and Alain Delon (eating). Trendy, touristy, but terrific ambience.

Aix-en-Provence
Information: 2 pl du Général-de-Gaulle (42.26.02.93).
Opening Times: Cézanne's Studio, Jun–Sep 10–12, 2.30–6; Oct–May 10–12, 2.30–5; closed Tue and public holidays.
Granet Museum, 10–12, 2–6 in season; closed Tue and public holidays.
St. Sauveur Cathedral, 8–12, 2–6.30.
Museum of Old Aix, 10–12, 2–6 in season; closed Mon and all Feb.
Festival: music, mid-Jul to mid-Aug.
Market: Tue, Thu and (best) Sat.
Hotel: Paul Cézanne, 40 av Victor-Hugo (42.26.34.73). Four-poster beds, friendly, near station. 44 rooms. No rest.
Restaurant: Aux Semailles, 15 rue Brueys (42.27.23.44). Intimate setting, Provençal specialities. Closed Mon. lunch and Sun.

Anduze
Information: plan de Brie (66 61 98 17).
Opening Times: Train à Vapeur des Cévennes, Easter and May–Sep. 40min run through splendid scenery to St. Jean-du-Gard (tickets, 66.85.13.17), 3 return steam train trips Thur–Sun in high season, otherwise mainly Sun.
Hotel: Les Trois Barbus, Le Roucan-Générargues, 4km N on D50. tel. 66.61.72.12. 36 rooms. Superb views, swimming pool, river, discounts for children. Closed Nov–Mar.

Ansouis
Opening Times: Château de Sabran, 2.30–6.30, closed Tue out of season: impressive collection of armour and tapestries, interesting gardens.
Mazoyer Museum, 2–6, 2–7 in season, closed Tue: shells and underwater sea life.
Restaurant: Hostellerie du Château, pl du Château (90.77.43.55). Unpretentious but substantial dishes.

Antibes
Information: pl du Général-de-Gaulle (93.33.95.64).
Opening Times: Picasso Museum, 8–12, 3–6 (3–7 in season), closed Tue, public holidays and all Nov.

Museum of Archaeology, 9–12, 2–6 (2–7 in season): Ancient Greek pottery from Antipolis.

Naval and Napoleonic Museum 10–12, 2–5 (3–7 in season). Closed Tue and Nov to mid-Dec: weapons, miniature soldiers, mementos.

Festival: St. Peter, 1st Sun after 29th Jun.

Hotel: Royal, bd du Maréschal-Leclerc (93.34.03.09). 43 rooms. Attractive private beach. Closed Nov to mid-Dec.

Restaurant: La Bonne Auberge, north of Antibes on Route Nationale 7 at la Brague (93.33.36.65; telex 470989). Breathtaking nouvelle cuisine and prices, megastar clientele, outside dining in summer.

Apt

Information: pl de la Bouquerie (90.74.03.18).

Opening Times: Former cathedral of Ste. Anne, sacristy, Jul–Aug 2.30–5, closed Sun, Mon.

Archaeological Museum, Mon, Wed–Sat (Sat am only) 10–12, 2.30–4.30 or 5.30 depending on season: an imposing 18th-century mansion with Roman remains and access to old Roman Arena.

Festival: Pilgrimage of Ste. Anne, last week in Jul.

Market: Sat.

Arles

Information: 35 pl de la République (90.96.29.35).

Opening Times: These have been standardised in Arles for most major sights to a minimum of 9–12, 2–7 in season, 9–12 and 2–4.30, and progressively later on longer days, out of season. All are closed 1st Jan, 1st May, 25th Dec. A single ticket is valid for les Alyscamps, the Arena, the Museums of Christian and Pagan Art, the Roman Theatre and cloister of St. Trophime.

The Museum Arlaten is open 9–12, 2–6 in season, and 2–4 or 5 out of season. Closed Mon.

St. Trophime church is open 10–12, 4–7.

Festival: des Gardiens, last Sun in Apr; music and drama, Jul.

Market: Sat.

Hotels: Jules César, 7 des Lices (90.93.43.20; telex 400239). Aptly sedate for former 17th-century Carmelite convent, but décor and restaurant outstanding. 60 rooms. Closed early Nov to mid-Dec.

D'Arlatan, 26 rue du Sauvage (90.93.56.66; telex 441203). Former 15th-century home of the Counts of Arlatan. Family run, elegant, enclosed garden (no rest.).

Restaurant: Le Vaccarès, enter by 9 rue Favorin (90.96.06.17). Fashionable, nouvelle cuisine, facing Roman forum.

Arpaillargues-et-Aureillac

Opening Times: Transport Museum open 9–12, 2–7, closed Mon., fine collection of cars and railway rolling stock.

Auribeau-sur-Siagne

Restaurant: Auberge Nossi-Bé (93.42.20.20). 6 rooms. Tiny auberge that does not take credit cards but with first-class, innovative restaurant. Hotel closed Jan to end-Feb. Restaurant also closed most Tue and (except high season) Wed.

Auron
Information: Immobilier la Ruade (93.23.02.66).
Hotel: Pilon, St. Étienne-de-Tinée (93.23.00.15). 30 rooms. Closed mid-Apr to late Jun, Sep to mid-Dec. Own skating rink. Poolside lunches in summer season.

Avignon
Information: 41 cours Jean-Jaurès (90.82.65.11).
Opening Times: Palace of the Popes Jul–Sep, 9–6; Oct–Easter, 9–11, 2–4; Easter–Jun, 9–11.30, 2–5.30.
St. Bénézet Bridge Jul–Aug 9–12, 2–7 (2–8, May, Jun, Sep; 2–5 Oct to mid-Jan and Mar). Closed Tue out of season, 1st Jan, 2–5 14th July, 25th Dec and mid-Jan to end Feb.
Museum of the Petit Palais, 9–11.30, 2–4. Closed Tue and public holidays.
Festival: International Drama, mid-July to early Aug.
Market: Mon–Sat and flea market on Sat.
Hotel: Europe, 12 pl Crillon (90.82.66.92; telex 431965). 53 rooms. Louis XV furniture in stylish 16th-century Avignon house where Napoléon once stayed — and left without paying, as was often his custom. Superb restaurant, closed Mon. lunch and many Sun.
Restaurant: Hiély-Lucullus, 5 rue de la République (90.86.17.07). Set menu, but what a menu, with multiple choices of brilliant, classic cuisine. Châteauneuf-du-Pape is the house wine. Closed Tue. Mon except in high season, mid-Jun to early Jul, Christmas and New Year.

Bagnols-sur-Cèze
Information: esplanade Mont-Cotton (66.89.54.61).
Market: Wed.

Bandol
Information: allées Vivien (94.29.41.35).
Opening Times: Parc Zoologique, 3km north-east close to A50 autoroute. Small zoo, small animals, ideal for children. 8–12 (except Sun), 2–7.
Hotel: Ker Mocotte, rue Raimu (94.29.46.53). 19 rooms. Former home of Toulon actor, Raimu. Private beach, special facilities for children. Closed mid-Oct to end Jan.
Restaurant: La Grotte Provençale, rue Docteur-Marcon (94.29.41.52). Good value Provençal cooking. Closed Tue eve and Wed except in high season and Dec to end-Jan.

La Barben
Opening Times: Castle, 10–12, 2–6, closed Tue, mid-Sep to Easter.
Hotels: La Touloubre (90.55.16.85). 17 rooms. Regional specialities in the restaurant, very good value. Hotel closed second half of Nov and of Jan, restaurant closed Sun eve and Mon.

Barbentane
Opening Times: Château, Easter to end-Oct, 10–12, 2–6. Closed Wed except high season. Sun only Nov–Easter, 10–12, 2–6.
Market: Mon–Sat.

Barcelonnette

Information: av de la Libération (92.81.04.71).
Market: Wed, Sat.
Restaurant: Les Blancs, Pra-Loup (92.84.16.60), 9km south-west on D902, D109. Exceptional value set-price meals and takeaways for campers.

Barjols

Festival: St. Marcel, every 4th year, closest Sun to 17th Jan.
Market: Tue, Thur, Sat.

Le Barroux

Opening Times: Château, open Jul to end-Aug, 10–12, 2–6.
Market: Apricot market Mon–Sat, July to end-Aug.

Les Baux

Information: Impasse du Château (90.97.34.39).
Opening Times: Entrance fee charged for deserted village and ruined castle, 9–8, otherwise free.
Museum of Modern Art, Porcelets Mansion, Easter to end-Oct, 9–12, 2–6.30. Closed Wed except high season.
Festival: Pageant of the Nativity, 24th Dec.
Hotels: Oustaù de Baumanière (90.54.33.07; telex 420203). 15 rooms. Provençal farmhouse north-west of Les Baux at foot of road leading to ruins. Luxurious rooms, world class cuisine, with prices to match. The wine cellar contains 35,000 magnificent bottles. Closed mid-Jan. to early March.La Benvengudo (90.54.32.54). 16 rooms. Informal, friendly farmhouse south-west of les Baux off D78f. Exceptional restaurant (closed lunchtime and Sun.). Closed Nov to end Jan.

Beauclaire

Information: 6 rue de l'Hôtel-de-Ville (66.59.26.57).
Opening Times: Castle, Apr–Sep, 10–12, 2–7; Oct–Mar, 10–12, 1.30–5.30. Closed Tue.
Vignasse Museum, 10–12, 2–6; historical collection in remains of old château.
Festival: commemorating medieval fair, end Jul to early Aug.
Market: Sun.

Beaulieu-sur-Mer

Information: pl de la Gare (93.01.02.21).
Opening Times Villa Kérylos, Jul–Aug, 3–7; Sep–Jun, 2–6; closed Mon, all Nov.
Festival: Folklore, 14th July.
Hotel: La Réserve, 5 bd Maréschal-Leclerc (93.01.00.01; telex 470301). 50 rooms. As the telephone number might suggest, almost the pioneer establishment to possess one, a century-old hotel still offering food and service in the grand manner. Closed Dec to early Jan.

Biot

Opening Times: Fernand Léger Museum, Mar–Oct, 10–12, 2–6; Nov–Feb, 10–12, 2–5. Closed Tue.
Hotels: Galerie des Arcades, 16 pl des Arcades (93.65.01.04). 12 rooms. 15th-

century atmospheric house, family run, fine Provençal cooking. Restaurant closed Sun eve, Mon, all Nov.

Bollène
Information: pl de la Mairie (90.30.14.43).
Market: Mon.
Festival: Parrot fair, Jun.

Bonnieux
Information: rue République (90.75.80.06).
Market: Sat.

Bormes-les-Mimosas
Information: rue Jean-Aicard (94.71.15.17) and av. Mer (94.64.82.57).
Market: flea market 1st Sat of month, alternate Sat in season.
Restaurant: La Tonnelle des Delices, pl Gambetta (94.71.34.84). Provençal cuisine, huge portions.

Brignoles
Information: pl St. Louis (94.69.01.78).
Opening Times: Palace of the Counts, now Regional Museum, Apr–Sep, 9–12, 2.30–6; 2–5. Oct–Mar, 10–12. Shorter hours Sun. Closed Mon, Tue and mid-Sep to mid-Oct: includes reconstruction of 18th-century Provençal kitchen.
Market: Sat.

Cagnes
Information: 26 av Renoir, Cagnes-sur-Mer (93.20.61.64).
Opening Times: Renoir Museum, av des Collettes, Cagnes-Ville, 10–1, 2–6. Closed Tue, mid-Oct to mid-Nov.
Château-Museum, le Haut-de-Cagnes, high season, 10–12, 2.30–7; rest of year, 10–12, 2–6. Closed Tue·except high season and mid-Oct to mid-Nov.
Festival: International Flower, Cagnes-sur-Mer, Easter.
Market: daily.
Restaurant: La Reserve, 91 bd de la Plage, Cros-de-Cagnes (93.31.00.17).
Hotel: Le Cagnard, rue du Pontis-Long, Haut-de-Cagnes, (93.20.73.22; telex 462223). 19 rooms, Converted 13th-century houses, superb terrace, stunning sea views. Parking is a problem.

Cannes
Information: Palais des Congres, la Croisette (93.39.24.53) and railway station (93.99.19.77).
Opening Times: Castre Museum, Apr–Jun, 10–12, 3–6; Jul–Sep 10–12, 3–7; Oct and mid-Dec to Mar, 10–12,2–5. Closed Tue, public holidays, Nov to mid-Dec: wide-ranging archaeological and ethnographic collection.
Boats to the Îles de Lérins (93.39.11.82): ten return trips daily in summer, five in winter. Île St. Honorat 30 min; Île Ste. Marguerite 15 min.
Monastery of St. Honorat, 10–4.30. Closed Good Friday.
Fort Royal, Ste. Marguerite, Apr–Sept 8–6; Oct–Mar 8–5. Closed early Jan to mid-Feb and mid-Jul to mid-Aug.

Festivals: Film, May; Yachting Regatta, Sep.
Hotels: Carlton, 58 la Croisette (93.68.91.68; telex 470720). 355 rooms. Luxury hotel in the grand manner, splendid views, private beach.
Gray d'Albion, 38 rue des Serbes (93.68.54.54; telex 470744). 200 rooms. Opulent, private beach, Royal Gray restaurant with incomparable dishes and prices.
Restaurant: La Brouette de Grand'Mere, 9 rue d'Oran (93.39.12.10). An oasis in a desert of inflated prices, single fixed menu and unlimited wine. No lunches. Closed Sun, first half of July, Nov to mid-Dec.

Carpentras
Information: av. Jean-Jaurès (90.63.00.78).
Opening Times: Comtadin Regional Museum, summer, 10–12, 2–6; winter, 10–12, 2–4, closed Wed.
Inguimbertine Library, 9.30–12, 2.30–7, closed Sat pm, all Sun, Mon am.
Festival: Music, mid-Jul to mid-Aug.
Market: Mon–Sat.

Cassis
Information: pl Baragnon (42.01.71.17).
Hotel: Les Roches Blanches, route de Port-Miou, 2km W of Cassis, (42.01.09.30; telex 441287). 36 rooms. Quiet, comfortable, family run, agreeable garden leading to seaside rocks. Closed Dec–Jan.

Castellane
Information: rue Nationale (92.83.61.14).
Festival: des Petardiers, 31st Jan.
Market: Wed, Sat.

Cavaillon
Information: rue Saunierie (90.71.32.01).
Opening Times: Archaeological museum, in high season, 10–12, 2–6; otherwise, 10–12, 3–5. Closed Tue.
Market: Mon.
Restaurant: Nicolet, 13 pl Gambetta (90.78.01.56). Superb home cooking, home-made pastries and desserts. Closed Sun, Mon, mid-Feb, early Jul.

Châteauneuf-du-Pape
Information: pl. Portail (90.83.71.08).
Festival: Wine-growers, 24th/25th Apr.
Hotel: Château Fines Roches, 2km south on D17 (90.83.70.23). 7 rooms. Exceptional restaurant. Restaurant closed Mon out of season. Hotel closed lated Dec to mid-Feb.
Restaurant: La Mule du Pape, 2 rue de la République (90.83.73.30). Regional specialities, fine cellar. Closed Mon eve and Tue, mid-Nov to mid-Feb.

Collobrières
Opening Times: Charterhouse of la Verne, Oct–Jun, 10–12, 2–6. Closed Tue.
Market: Sun.

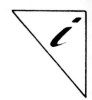

Colmars-les-Alpes
Information: Hôtel des Postes (92.83.41.92).

Cucuron
Market: daily.

Cuges-les-Pins
Opening Times: On N8, midway (32km) between Marseille and Toulon, the OK Corral, Apr–Sep, 10–6.30, Mar–Oct, weekends 10–6, closed Nov to end-Feb. Wild West amusement park with out-of-work actors.

Digne-les-Bains
Information: Le Rond-Point (92.31.42.73).
Festival: Lavender, first Sun in Aug.
Market: Wed, Sat.
Hotel: Grand Paris, 19 bd Thiers (92.31.11.15; telex 430605). 37 rooms. 17th-century monastery converted into hotel of considerable character and with an exceptional restaurant. Hotel closed Jan to end-Feb, restaurant Sun eve and Mon.

Draguignan
Information: 9 bd Clemenceau (94.68.63.30).
Opening Times: Museum and Library, 9–12, 2–6; closed Tue and public holidays: 14th-century illuminated manuscript of the *Roman de la Rose*, a tale of chivalry.
Market: Wed, Sat; flea market first Sat each month.

Entrecasteaux
Opening Times: Château, Apr–Sep, 10–8; Oct–Mar, 10–6.

Entrevaux
Information: at the mairie (93.05.40.04).
Festival: 16th/17th-century music, first half Aug.

Èze
Information: at the mairie (93.41.03.03).
Opening Times: Jardin Exotique, 9–sunset: multiple cacti and other exotic plants; superb coastal views.
Hotel: Château de la Chèvre d'Or, rue Barri (93.41.12.12; telex 970839). 8 rooms. 11th-century château, antique furnishings, even the phones. Sea views, exquisite restaurant, full of the rich and the famous. Hotel closed Dec to end Feb. Restaurant also closed Wed Oct–Easter.
Restaurant: Le Nid d'Aigle, 1 rue du Château (93.43.19.08). Local fare, friendly, good value. Closed Thur and mid-Nov to mid-Dec.

Fontaine-de-Vaucluse
Information: pl de l'Église (90.20.32.22).
Opening Times: Free access to the source of the spring.
Petrarch Museum, mid-Apr to mid-Oct, 9.30–12, 2–6.30; rest of year, weekends only: fine collection of Petrarch's works.
Norbert Casteret museum, Jun to end-Aug, 9–12, 2–6.30, otherwise Feb to end-Oct, Wed–Sun, 10–12, 2–6.30. Closed Nov to end-Jan: speleology, amidst impres-

sive stalactites, relating subterranean exploration of the Sorge.
Vallis Clausa, paper mill, summer, 9–7; winter, 9–12.30, 2–6 (Sun 10–12.30, 2–6).
Festival: of the Sorgue, Jul.
Market: Tue.

Fontvieille
Information: at the mairie (90.97.70.01).
Opening Times: Daudet's Mill, 2km south, Apr–Sep 8.30–12, 1–5.30.
Market: Mon, Fri.
Hotel: La Regalido, rue Frédéric-Mistral (90.97.60.22; telex 441150). 11 rooms. Converted ancient oil mill, immaculate gardens, outstanding classic cuisine. Hotel closed Dec to mid-Jan. Restaurant also closed all Mon, Tue lunch.

Forcalquier
Information: pl du Bourguet (92.75.10.02).
Opening Times: Convent des Cordeliers, May, Jun, 2.30–6.30; Jul, Aug, 10–12, 2.30–6.30. Otherwise often closed: 12th-century, one of the earliest Franciscan monasteries in France.
Market: Mon.
Hotel: Deux Lions, 11 pl du Bourguet (92.75.25.30). 18 rooms. 17th-century coach house, still taking the passing trade. Excellent restaurant. Hotel closed Jan to mid-Feb. Restaurant also closed Sun eve and Mon.

Fox-Amphoux
Hotel: Auberge de Vieux Fox (94.80.71.69). 10 rooms. Former church presbytery, delightful if tiny bedrooms, splendid terrace. Quiet, friendly, good restaurant. Closed late Dec to mid-Feb.

Fréjus
Information: pl du Docteur-Calvini, Fréjus (94.51.53.87) and bd de la Libération, Fréjus-Plage (94.51.48.42).
Opening Times: Amphitheatre, baptistery, cloister and archaeological museum, summer, 9.30–12, 2–6; winter, 9.30–12, 2–4.30. Closed Tue, public holidays.
Festival: bravade, third Sun after Easter.
Market: Wed, Sat.

La Garde-Freinet
Opening Times: Jean Aicard Museum, 10–12, 2–6: commemorating the 19th-century romantic novelist who lived here and wrote *Mauris des Maures.*
Restaurant: Faücado, bd de l'Esplanade (94.43.60.41). Local cooking, charming setting, fine views over the valley. Closed Tue and mid-Nov to mid-Dec.

Gassin
Restaurant: Bello Visto, pl des Barrys (94.56.17.30). Eat under the shade of large leafy trees with superb view of the Mediterranean far below. Fine local cooking.

Gémenos
Hotel: Relais de la Magdeleine, Gémenos (42.82.20.05). 20 rooms. 17th-century country house on outskirts of town, swimming pool, fine local cuisine, no credit cards, discounts for children. Closed Dec–Feb.

Giens

Hotel: Relais du Bon Accueil, Giens (94.58.20.48). 10 rooms. Secluded hotel on headland with superb sea views, though some rooms extremely small. Closed mid-Nov to early Dec. No credit cards.

Gordes

Information: pl du Château (90.72.02.75).
Opening Times: Château and Vasarély Museum, 10–12, 2–6. Closed Tue.
Village des Bories, 3km south-west, Feb to mid-Nov 9–sunset; mid-Nov to Jan weekends 10–sunset. Moulin des Bouillons, 5km south, 10–12, 2–6.
Festival: Music and Theatre, first half Aug.
Market: Tue.
Hotel: Domaine de l'Enclos, route de Sénanque (90.72.08.22; telex 432119). 14 rooms. Network of tiny cottages cunningly disguises first-class amenities and fine restaurant. Hotel closed Nov to mid-Mar. Restaurant also closed Mon.
Restaurant: Les Bories, rte de l'Abbaye de Sénanque (90.72.00.51). Exceptional cuisine in group of ancient *bories* on stony plateau. You can stay, too. Closed Sun, Mon, Tue eves, all Wed, and late Nov to end Dec. Booking essential.

Gourdon

Information: at the mairie (93.42.50.17).
Opening Times: Château-Museum, Jul to mid-Sep, 11–1, 2–7; mid-Sep to end-Jun, 10–12, 2–7. Closed Tue.

Grasse

Information: pl Foux (93 36 03 56).
Opening Times: Fragonard Perfume Factory, May to end-Oct, Mon–Sat 8.30–6.30, Sun 9–12, 2–18; Nov to end-Apr 9–12, 2–6.
Fragonard Villa-Museum, 10–12, 2–6 (2–5 in winter), closed Sat, some Sun, all Nov.
Marine Museum, 2.30–5; exploits of Admiral Count de Grasse.
Festival: Music and Drama, second half Jul.
Market: Mon–Sat.
Restaurant: Maitre Boscq, 13 rue de la Fontette (93.36.45.76). Local specialities in cramped, congenial atmosphere. No credit cards.

Grimaud

Information: pl des Écoles (94.43.26.78).
Hotel: Hostellerie du Côteau Fleuri, place des Pénitents (94.43.20.17). Quiet auberge, fine views, local specialities. Closed Nov to mid-Mar.
Restaurant: Les Santons, called after the clay figurines representing archetypes of Provençal life, offers typical Provençal décor and a brilliant menu and cellar. Route Nationale (94.43.21.02).

Hyères

Information: pl Clemenceau (94.65.18.55).
Opening Times: to the Îles d'Hyères, boats leave from la Tour Fondue on the Giens peninsula, 6 daily summer crossings to Porquerolles, 30min (94.58.21.81); from

Port d'Hyères, daily summer crossing to Port-Cros (94.57.44.07).
Market: third Thu of each month.
Hotels: Mas du Langoustier, Porquerolles (94.58.30.09). 48 rooms. Superb views, considerable restaurant. Closed late Sep to early May.
Le Manoir, Port-Cros (94.05.90.52). 24 rooms. 18th-century manor, country house atmosphere, many famous visitors, essential to book four or five months in advance.

L'Isle-sur-la-Sorgue
Information: pl de l'Église (90.38.04.78).
Opening Times: Old Hospital, Jun to end-Sep, Mon–Sat 10–12, 2–6.
Festival: of the Sorgue, last week Jul.
Market: Thu and (especially) Sun.

Isola 2000
Information: maison d'Isola (93.02.70.50).

Juan-les-Pins
Information: bd Charles-Guillaumont (93.61.04.98).
Festival: International Jazz, second half Jul.
Hotels: Belles-Rives, bd Baudoin (93.61.02.79; telex 470984). 44 rooms. Luxurious establishment next to own private beach and private jetty, delightful terrace. Closed Oct to near Easter.
Juana, av Gallica (93.61.08.70; telex 470778). 50 rooms. Sedate luxury, though away from own private beach. Brilliant restaurant, La Terrasse with outdoor terrace, closed for lunch Jul–Aug. Hotel closed Oct to near Easter.

Le Lavandou
Information: quai Gabriel-Péri (94.71.00.61).
Opening Times: daily summer service to Port-Cros and Île de Levant (94.71.01.02).
Festival: St. Jean, 29th Jun.
Restaurant: Au Vieux Port, quai Gabriel-Peri (94.71.00.21). Fish specialities. Closed mid-Jan to mid-Mar; Sun eve, Tue except in season.

Lourmarin
Opening Hours: château, summer, 9–11.45, 2.30–5.45; winter, 9–11.45, 2.30–4.45. Closed Tue (Oct–Apr).

Le-Luc-en-Provence
Information: pl de Verdun (94.60.74.51); or at the mairie (94.60.88.21).
Festival: Cherry, third Sun in May.
Market: Fri.
Hotel: Parc, 12 rue Jean-Jaurès (94.60.70.01). 12 rooms. Excellent restaurant, closed Mon eve and Tue. Hotel closed early May, mid-Nov to mid-Dec.

Maillane
Opening Times: Mistral Museum, Jun to end-Sep, 9–12, 2–6; Apr, Oct, 10–12, 2–5; Nov to end-Mar, 10–12, 2–4.
Festival: St.-Agatha, first Sun after 4th Feb.

Manosque
Information: pl Docteur Paul-Joubert (92.72.16.00).
Market: Sat.
Restaurant: Hostellerie de la Fuste (92.72.05.95) 6km south-east. Exceptional local dishes, served on delightful terrace. Also hotel. Closed Sun eve and Mon, early Jan to late Feb.

Marseille
Information: 4 la Canebière (91.54.91.11).
Opening Times: Marine Museum, 10–12, 2.30–6, closed Tue.
Roman Docks Museum, 10–12, 2.30–6, closed all Tue and Wed am.
Marseille Historical Museum, 12–7, closed Sun, Mon.
Fine Arts Museum, 10–12, 2–6.15, closed all Tue, Wed am. Museum of Archaeology (Château Borély), 9.30–12.15, 1–5.30. Closed all Tue and Wed am.
Festival: Santons Fair, 2 weeks from first Sun in Nov.
Market: daily.
Hotel: Le Petit Nice, 160 Corniche John F. Kennedy (91.52.14.39; telex 401565). 19th-century villa on rocky headland, elegant, comfortable. 20 rooms including Marina Maldormé, for once, a superior annex. Outstanding restaurant Passédat, closed Mon. Hotel closed Jan.
Restaurant: Aux Mets de Provence, 18, quai de Rive-Neuve (91.33.35.38). Eccentric, brilliant, single but prodigious menu, expensive. No smokers. Booking essential. Closed Sun, Mon.

Martigues
Information: quai Paul-Doumer (42.80.30.72).
Festival: Jousting, first Sun in Jul.

Ménerbes
Hotel: Le Roi Soleil, route des Baumettes (90.72.25.61). 14 rooms. Comfortable, friendly, creative restaurant, closed Tue lunch. Hotel closed mid-Nov to mid-Mar.
Restaurant: Pascal (90.72.22.13). Country cooking, massive set menu, great local favourite, lunches only. Closed Nov–Easter.

Menton
Information: Palais de l'Europe, av Boyer (93.57.57.00).
Opening Times: Municipal Museum, mid-Jun to mid-Sept, 10–12, 3–6.30; rest of year, 10–12, 2–5.30. Closed Nov.
Festivals: Lemon, Feb/Mar; Chamber Music, Aug.
Market: daily; flea-market on Fri.
Restaurant: Auberge les Santons, colline de l'Annonciade (93.35.94.10). Hilltop views, superb nouvelle cuisine. Also a hotel (10 rooms). Closed mid-Nov to mid-Dec.

Meyrargues
Market: Wednesday.
Hotel: Château de Meyrargues (42.57.50.32). 14 rooms. 12th-century château overlooking the village turned into plush hotel with incredible ambience: the

children will love it, but keep them off the Louis XV furniture. Closed Dec to end-Jan.

Monaco
Information: 2a bd des Moulins, Monte Carlo (93.30.87.01).
Opening Times: Prince's Palace, Jun–Sep, 9.30–6.30, 1st–15th Oct 10–5. Closed rest of year and when Prince in residence.
Festival: International Television, Feb; Formula One Grand Prix, May.
Hotels: Hermitage, sq Beaumarchais, Monte Carlo (93.50.67.31; telex 479432). 260 rooms. Classified historic monument, amazing décor includes domed winter garden foyer, huge period bedrooms. Restaurant Belle Epoque in sumptuous Baroque with superb classic cuisine.
Paris, pl du Casino, Monte Carlo (93.50.80.80; telex 469925). 255 rooms. Private passage to Les Terrasses bathing centre. Slightly faded grandeur and déclassé clientele, rooftop grill, and revived Le Louis XIV restaurant with superb specialities.
Restaurant: Sam's Place, 1 av Henri-Dunant (93.50.89.33). You cannot eat cheaply in Monte Carlo but this vivacious brasserie has better prices than most. Closed Sun.

Mougins
Information: pl du Commandant-Lamy (93.75.82.83).
Restaurants: Le Moulin des Mougins, 424 chemin de Moulin, 2km south-east on D3 (93.75.78.24; telex 970732). Probably the best restaurant in Provence, inspired cuisine, great wines, and prices to match. 5 luxurious bedrooms if you book years ahead. Instantly recognisable clientele. Closed all Mon, Thu lunch, except high season, early Feb to late Mar, early Nov to mid-Dec.
Feu Follet, pl du Commandant-Lamy (93.90.15.78). The other end of the spectrum to Le Moulin, but excellent fare at reasonable prices: do not expect to linger. Closed all Mon, Sun eve out of season, early Nov to late Mar.
Hotel: Le Mas Candille, bd Rebuffel just west of village, (93.90.00.85; telex 462131). 25 rooms. 17th-century Provençal mas, front room with good views, excellent nouvelle cuisine, swimming pool. Closed Nov–Dec.

Moustiers-Ste.-Marie
Information: High season only (94.74.67.84).
Opening Times: Faïence Museum, Jun to end-Aug, 9–12, 2–7; rest of year, 10–12, 2–6. Closed Nov–Mar.
Market: Fri.
Restaurant: Les Santons, pl de l'Église (92.74.66.48). Provençal specialities in breathtaking environment. Closed Mon eve and all Tue except high season, early Jan to end-Mar.

La Napoule
Information: rue Jean-Aulas, la Napoule (93.49.95.31) or av de Cannes, Mandelieu-la-Napoule (93.49.14.39).
Opening Times: Henry Clews castle, depends on exhibitions but guided tours usually at 4, 5. Closed Tue and most Dec.
Restaurant: L'Oasis, rue Jean-Honoré Carle (93.49.95.52). A rival to Le Moulin des

Mougins, one of the great restaurants of France, memorable dining on the patio of a white villa dominated by its majestic palm tree.

Nice
Information: av Thiers (93.87.07.07) and 5 av Gustave-V (93.87.60.60). Recorded information in English (93.85.65.83).
Opening Times: Masséna Museum, May–Sept, 9–12, 3–6; Oct–Apr, 10–12, 2–5. Closed Mon and public holidays.
Jules Chéret Fine Arts Museum, high season, 10–12, 2–6, otherwise 10–12, 2–5; 17th-, 18th–20th-century French painters.
Matisse Museum, May–Sep, 10–12, 2.30–6.30; Oct–Apr, 10–12, 2–5. Closed all Mon, Sun am, all Nov.
Festival: Carnival, 2 weeks before Lent; Battle of Flowers, day following Ash Wednesday; Music, May and Oct.
Market: daily. Flower market 6–5.30 daily except Sun am and all Mon.
Hotels: Negresco, 37 promenade des Anglais (93.88.39.51; telex 460040). 150 rooms. Décor from days of the Empire and Napoléon III, wonderful ambience and service, private beach opposite, brilliant Restaurant Chantecler.
La Pérouse, 11 quai Rauba-Capéu (93.62.34.63). A lift takes guests to reception, halfway up the empty château hill. Bedrooms, some with kitchenettes, have superb views over the bay below. Lunchtime grills by the pool, otherwise eat out. Restaurant closed Nov. Mercure, 2 rue Halévy, tel. 93.82.30.88. 124 rooms, but only those overlooking Promenade des Anglais worth having: they integrate with adjacent more costly hotel, so the people above may be paying double. No restaurant.
Restaurant: Le Bistrot d'Antoine, 26 bd Victor-Hugo (93.88.49.75). Local specialities at bargain prices. Closed Sun.

Nîmes
Information: 6 rue Auguste (66.67.29.11).
Opening Times: Maison Carrée, Temple of Diana, Tour Magna, summer, 9–12, 2–7; winter, 9–12, 2–5. Closed Sun pm and May 1.
Amphitheatre, summer, 9–7; winter, 9–5.
Festival: Pentecost (bullfights, concerts, dancing), Whitsun.
Market: flowers and antiques, Mon; flea market, Sun.
Restaurant: Au Cocotier, 15 rue Pierre-Sernard (66.67.83.29). Unusual selection of dishes from former French island possessions. Closed Sun, all Aug.

Noves
Information: at the Mairie (90.94.14.01).
Hotel: Auberge de Noves (90.94.19.21; telex 431312). 22 rooms. Off D28, 3km west of Noves, convenient Avignon airport. 19th-century manor house set in woodlands, family run, superb suites, magnificent food, exquisite service.

Orange
Information: av du Ch.-de-Gaulle (90.34.70.88).
Opening Times: Theatre, 9–6.30 except on days of performances.
Festival: Music, last two weeks Jul.

Restaurant: Le Bec Fin, 14 rue Segond-Weber (90.34.13.76). Provençal dishes, conveniently close to the Roman Theatre. Closed Thu, Fri eve, all Nov.

Pégomas
Hotel: Le Bosquet, quartier du Château (93.42.22.87). 25 rooms, including some in villas in the grounds complete with kitchenettes (otherwise eat out). Friendly service, quiet atmosphere, swimming pool. No credit cards.

Peillon
Hotel: Auberge de la Madone (93.79.91.17). 18 rooms. Former nunnery, quiet, beautiful views, ingenious cuisine. Closed 1st week Jun, mid-Oct to mid-Dec. No credit cards.

Pernes-les-Fontaines
Market: Sat; daily asparagus market in summer.

Peyrolles-en-Provence
Market: Wed; daily Apr–Jun.

Pont-St.-Esprit
Information: la Citadelle (66.39.13.25).

Port Grimaud
Hotel: Giraglia, pl du 14 Juin (94.56.31.33; telex 470494). 48 rooms. An integral part of the artificial town, elegant bedrooms, swimming pool, private beach. Closed mid-Oct to Easter.

Roquebrune-Cap-Martin
Information: av. P.-Doumer (93.35.62.87) and esplanade Jean-Giono (93.57.99.44).
Opening Hours: Château-Museum, summer, 9–12, 2–7; winter, 10–12, 2–5, closed Fri: only surviving Carolingian fortress in France.
Festival: Entombment of Christ, Good Friday; Christ's Passion, 5th Aug.
Hotel: Vista Palace, Grand Corniche (93.35.01.50; telex 461021). 27 rooms. Luxury hotel on cliff top high above the sea, outstanding service, excellent restaurant Le Vistaero. Closed Nov to end-Mar.

La Roque-sur-Cèze
Restaurant: Le Mas du Belier, Mas Pont (66.82.79.73). Lovely location on terrace beside the river Cèze, overlooking the hill village. Family run, friendly service.

Roussillon
Information: pl de la Poste.
Market: Wed.

St.-Etienne-de-Tinée
Information: 1 rue des Communes-de-France (93.02.41.96).
Market: Sun.

St.-Jean-Cap-Ferrat
Information: 59 av Denis-Semeria (93.01.36.86).

Opening Hours: Ephrussi de Rothschild Villa, July–Aug, 3–7; Sep, Oct, Dec–Jun, 2–6; closed Nov. Gardens only, 9–12.

Zoo, May–Sep, 9.30–6.30; Oct–Apr, 9.30–5.30.

Hotel: Voile d'Or au Port (93.01.13.13; telex 470317). 50 rooms. Luxurious, beautiful harbour setting with two swimming pools beside the sea and an outstanding restaurant with, as might be expected, fish specialities.

St.-Maximin-la-Ste.-Baume
Information: Hôtel de Ville (94.78.00.09).
Opening Times: Basilica of Ste.-Marie-Madeleine, 8–11.45, 2–7.
Festival: Ste.-Madeleine, 21st/22nd July; Music, Aug.
Market: daily.

St.-Paul-de-Vence
Information: Maison Tour, rue Grande (93.32.86.95).
Opening Times: Maeght Foundation, May–Sept, 10–12.30, 3–7; Oct–Apr, 10–12.30, 2.30–6.
Festival: Music, second half Jul.
Hotels: La Colombe d'Or, 1 pl du Général-de-Gaulle (93.32.80.02; telex 970607). 24 rooms. Luxury hotel, legendary art collection, agreeable cuisine. Closed early Nov to mid-Dec.
Mas d'Artigny, chemin des Salettes (93.32.84.54; telex 470601). 81 rooms, including 26 villa suites, swimming pool, lido, every conceivable luxury. Outstanding restaurant with excellent regional dishes.
Restaurant: La Belle-Epoque, Route de Cagnes, la Colle-sur-Loup, 5km south (93.20.10.92). Creative turn-of-the-century setting, classic cuisine. Closed Mon and early Jan to mid-Feb.

St.-Raphaël
Information: pl de la Gare (94.95.16.87).
Festival: Traditional Jazz, Jul.
Market: daily.
Hotel: La Potinière, Routes des Plaines, Boulouris (94.95.21.43). 25 rooms. Leafy suburb by the sea, accent on youth, hotel has own motor yacht complete with crew. Closed early Nov to late Dec, Thurs out of season.

St.-Rémy-de-Provence
Information: pl Jean-Jaurès (90.92.05.22).
Opening Times: ruins of Glanum 2km south, in season, 9–12, 2–6; out of season, 10–12, 2–5.
Festival: Provençal, 15th Aug.
Market: daily.
Hotels: Château de Roussan, route de Tarascon, about 2km west (90.92.11.63). 12 rooms. 18th-century château taking paying guests for bed and breakfast. Superb ambience, wonderful gardens ... and modern plumbing. Advance booking essential. Reverts to private use mid-Oct to mid-Mar.
Hotel Van Gogh, 1 avenue Jean-Moulin (90.92.14.02). 18 rooms. On outskirts of town, modern, comfortable, swimming pool, no rest.

Restaurant: Le Castelet des Alpilles, 6 pl Mireille (90.92.07.21). Traditional Provençal cuisine served on agreeable terrace, also hotel. Closed mid-Nov to end Feb.

St.-Tropez

Information: quai Jean-Jaurès (94.97.45.21).

Opening Times: Annonciade Museum, Jun–Sep, 10–12, 2–7; Oct–May, 10–12, 2–6. Closed Tue and all Nov.

Festival: bravade of St.-Tropez, 16th/17th May; Fête des Españols, 15th Jun.

Market: Tue, Sat.

Hotel: Byblos, av Paul-Signac (94.97.00.04; telex 470235). 107 rooms. Built like a Provençal hill village with little alleyways and patios grouped around the central swimming pool, its ingenuity is matched by its opulent furnishings, exemplary service, and brilliant nouvelle cuisine of its restaurant, le Chabichou, in the av Foch (94.54.80.00). This is where the guest list reads like a Hollywood film credits. Byblos closes Nov to end-Mar. Le Chabichou mid-Oct to mid-May.

Restaurant: Café des Arts, pl des Lices (94.97.02.25). Mediocre food, but the ambience, my dear, the ambience ... Closed Oct to end-Mar.

Les-Stes.-Maries-de-la-Mer

Information: av Van Gogh (90.47.82.55). Camargue information centre 5km north at Ginès (90.97.86.32).

Opening Times: Ste.-Madeleine crypt, Apr–Sep, 7.30–12, 2–7.30; Oct–Mar, 9–6.

Festival: Gipsy pilgrimage, 24th/25th May (also weekend nearest 22nd Oct and first Sun in Dec).

Market: Mon, Fri.

Hotels: Mas de la Fouque, route d'Aigues-Mortes, 5km north-west (90.47.81.02). 10 rooms. Ranch hotel, riding facilities into the Camargue, but heated swimming pool, dazzlingly appointed bathrooms and first-class food for anyone who does not really want to rough it. Closed mid-Nov to end-Mar.

L'Etrier Camarguais, chemin bas des Launes, route d'Arles, 3km N.(90.47.81.14). 28 rooms, some in chalets. Ranch hotel, riding, swimming pool, disco. Closed Nov–Mar.

Ste.-Maxime

Information: promenade Simon-Lozière (94.96.19.24).

Opening Times: St. Donat Park, 9½km north Easter–Oct, 10–12, 3–6.30: Museum of Gramophones including Edison's first. Closed rest of year.

Market: Mon–Sat.

Hotel: Calidianus, boulevard Jean Moulin, quartier de la Croisette, tel. 94.96.23.21. On hill to west of town overlooking the bay, modern, swimming pool, no credit cards, no rest. 27 rooms.

Salon-de-Provence

Information: 56 cours Gimon (90.56.27.60).

Opening Times: House of Nostradamus, 10–12, 3–7. Closed Tue.

Festival: Theatre, Jul and Aug.

Market: Wed.

Hotel: Abbaye de Ste.-Croix, route du Val-de-Cuech, 5km north-east (90.56.24.55; telex 401247). 12th-century abbey stuffed with antiques and precarious stone stairs. Tremendous atmosphere, but children safer elsewhere. Excellent restaurant with generous proportions, closed for Mon lunch. Hotel closed Nov to end-Feb.

Saorge
Information: at the mairie in Fontan (where you must go for access to Saorge) (90.04.50.01).

Sénanque
Opening Hours: Cistercian Abbey, Jun–Sep, 10–7; Oct–May, 10–12, 2–6.

Séguret
Festival: Provençal, second half of Aug (*bravade* on third Sun in Aug).
Hotels: La Table du Comtat, tel. 90.46.91.49. 8 rooms. 15th-century house, wonderful views, exceptional restaurant, small pool. Hotel closed mid-Jan to end-Feb. Restaurant closed Tue eve and Wed, except in high season. Bellerive, at Rasteau, north-west (90.46.10.20). 20 rooms. Modern, swimming pool, no credit cards. Closed Jan–Feb.

Seillans
Information: Le Valat (94.76.85.91).
Hotels: des Deux Rocs, place Font d'Amont, tel. 94.76.87.32. 15 rooms. In upper part of perched village west of Grasse, 18th-century mansion, splendid fountain, friendly, no credit cards. Closed Nov to late Mar. Château de Trigance, Trigance, 20km north-west (94.76.91.18). 8 rooms. In perched village, crenellated (but modern) château, hillside views, terrace, convenient for Gorges de Verdon. Closed Nov to late Mar.

Sérignan-du-Comtat
Opening Times: Fabre Museum, 10–12, 2–5. Closed Tue.

Silvacane
Opening Times: Cistercian Abbey, Apr–Sep, 10–12, 2–6.30; Oct–Mar, 10–12, 2–5. Closed Tue, Wed and public holidays.

Sisteron
Information: rue des Arcades (92.61.12.03).
Opening Times: Citadel, 9–7. Closed mid-Nov to mid-Mar: massive 13th-century construction strengthened to 16th-century; superb views.
Festival: Music and Theatre, mid-Jul to mid-Aug.
Hotel: La Bonne Etape, chemin du Lac, Châteaux-Arnoux, 14½km south-west (92.64.00.09; telex 430605). Former coach inn now sumptuous hotel with superb restaurant. Closed Sun eve and Mon. Hotel closed early Jan to mid-Feb, late Nov.

Tarascon
Information: av de la République (90.91.03.52).
Opening Times: Château, Apr–Sep, 9–12, 2–7, Oct–Mar, 10–12, 2–6. Closed Tue.
Festival: of the Tarasque, last Sun in Jun.
Market: Tue.

Tavel
Hotel: Auberge de Tavel, tel. 66.50.03.41. 11 rooms. Provençal mas in wine village north-west of Avignon, swimming pool, outstanding food . . . and try the rosé. Hotel closed Feb, restaurant closed Mon. out of season.

Le Thor
Opening Times: Thouzon Grotto, 3km north, Oct–Easter, 2–6; rest of year, 9–7.

Le Thoronet
Opening Times: Cistercian Abbey, May–Sep, 10–12, 2–6; Mar, Apr, Oct, 10–12, 2–5; Nov–Feb, 10–12, 2–4. Closed Tue.

Toulon
Information: 8 av Colbert (94.22.08.22), rue Mirabeau (94.93.01.18).
Opening Times: Art and Archaeological Museum, 10–12, 3–6. Closed Mon, Thu: 13th-to 20th-century paintings.
Tour Royale, Jun to mid-Sep, 2–7; mid-Sept to end-Oct, 2–6; Mar to end May, 3–6. Closed Mon, Nov to end-Feb.
Festival: Flower, Apr; Music, Jul; Circus Artists, Aug; Santons fair, Nov.
Market: daily; flea market on Sun.
Restaurant: Le Lutrin, 8 littoral Frédéric-Mistral (94.42.43.43). 19th-century villa in suburbs, facing the sea. Elegant, fastidious cuisine. Closed Sat.

La Tour d'Aigues
Market: Tue.

Tourtour
Restaurant: Chênes Verts, on 51 towards Villecroze (94.70.55.06). Tiny restaurant, booking essential; inspired cooking. No credit cards. Closed Jan–mid-Feb, Sun eve, Mon.

La Turbie
Information: at the mairie (93.41.10.10).

Uzès
Information: av de la Libération (66.22.68.88).
Opening Hours: Ducal Palace, summer, 9–12, 2–6; winter, 10–12, 2.30–5.
Festival: Garlic, 24th June; Wine, first and second Sat in Aug.
Market: Wed.
Hotel: Marie d'Agoult, château d'Arpaillargues, Arpaillargues, 5km west (66.22.14.48; telex 490415). 25 rooms, 2 apartments. 18th-century mansion, beautifully furnished, with a large swimming pool and a restaurant which, on good days, serves elegant, classic cuisine. Closed Nov to mid-Mar.

Vaison-la-Romaine
Information: pl de l'Abbé-Sautel (90.36.02.11).
Opening Hours: Roman ruins, Jul–Sep, 9–7; Mar–May, Oct, 9–6; Nov–Feb, 9–5.
Festival: Music and Theatre, mid-Jul to mid-Aug; Provençal, first Sun after 15th Aug.
Market: daily.
Hotel: Le Beffroi, rue de l'Évêché, Haute Ville (90.36.04.71). 21 rooms. 16th-

century mansion with quaint ceilings and floors, family-run, friendly atmosphere, agreeable terraced restaurant. Closed mid-Nov to mid-Dec, early Jan to mid-Mar.

Valbonne
Information: bd Gambetta (93.42.04.16).
Restaurant: Auberge Fleurie (93.42.01.80). Exceptional meals, agreeable terrace. Some rooms. Closed Wed and mid-Dec to early Feb.

Vallauris
Information: av des Martyrs-de-la-Resistance (93.63.82.58).
Opening Times: Picasso Museum, Apr–Oct, 10–12, 2–6; Nov–Mar, 10–12, 2–5. Ceramics and Modern Art Museum, 10–12, 2–5. Closed Tue.
Market: daily.

Vence
Information: pl du Grand-Jardin (93.58.06.38).
Opening Times: Rosary (Matisse) Chapel, Tue, Thu, 10–11.30, 2.30–5.30.
Festival: International Music, Jul; Battle of Flowers, Easter Sun and Mon.
Market: daily.
Hotels: Château du Domain St.-Martin, Route de Coursegoules, 3km north-west via D2 (93.58.02.02; telex 470282). 15 rooms, 10 luxurious villa apartments. Exquisite hotel lavishly appointed, heart-shaped swimming pool, prodigious views, stunning restaurant: all for those for whom money is no object. Hotel closed late Nov to end-Feb. Restaurant closed Wed out of season. Diana, avenue des Poilus (93.58.28.56). 25 rooms, each with kitchenette. Modern, central, no rest.

Villefranche-sur-Mer
Information: Jardin François-Binon (93.01.73.68).
Opening Times: Chapel St. Pierre, mid-June to mid-Sept, 9–12, 2.30–7 mid-Sept to mid-June, 9–12, 2–4.30. Closed Fri, mid-Nov to mid-Dec.

Villeneuve-lès-Avignon
Information: pl. Ch-David (90.25.61.33).
Opening Times: Val de Bénédiction Charterhouse, Apr–Sep, 10–12.30, 3–7.30; Oct–Mar, 10–12, 2–5. Closed Tue.
St. André Fort, Apr–Sep, 9–12, 2–6.30; rest of year, 10–12, 2–3. Closed public holidays.
Philip-le-Bel Tower, Apr–Sep, 9–12.30, 3–7; rest of year, 10–12, 2–5. Closed Tue and public holidays.
Festival: St.-Marc, end Apr.
Hotel: La Magnaneraie, 37 rue Camp-de-Bataille (90.25.11.11). 21 rooms. 15th-century inn on hillside outside Villeneuve, swimming pool, interesting local cuisine.

Villeneuve-Loubet
Information: at the mairie (93.20.20.09).

Opening Times: Auguste Escoffier gastronomic museum, 2–6; closed Mon and public holidays.
Festival: St.-Eloi, 20th/21st Jul.

Index